ISBN 978-0-656-60443-2
PIBN 11336404

1 MONTH OF FREE READING

at

www.ForgottenBooks.com

By purchasing this book you are eligible for one month membership to ForgottenBooks.com, giving you unlimited access to our entire collection of over 1,000,000 titles via our web site and mobile apps.

To claim your free month visit:

www.forgottenbooks.com/free1336404

English
Français
Deutsche
Italiano
Español
Português

www.forgottenbooks.com

Mythology Photography **Fiction**
Fishing Christianity **Art** Cooking
Essays Buddhism Freemasonry
Medicine **Biology** Music **Ancient
Egypt** Evolution Carpentry Physics
Dance Geology **Mathematics** Fitness
Shakespeare **Folklore** Yoga Marketing
Confidence Immortality Biographies
Poetry **Psychology** Witchcraft
Electronics Chemistry History **Law**
Accounting **Philosophy** Anthropology
Alchemy Drama Quantum Mechanics
Atheism Sexual Health **Ancient History**
Entrepreneurship Languages Sport
Paleontology Needlework Islam
Metaphysics Investment Archaeology
Parenting Statistics Criminology
Motivational

Historic, Archive Document

Do not assume content reflects current
scientific knowledge, policies, or practices.

The Roses of New Castle

1929

New Rose
"Pride of
New Castle"

See
page two

HELLER BROS. COMPANY
P. J. LYNCH, Owner
NEW CASTLE, INDIANA

PHILIPPINE ISLANDS. All the roses purchased from you are growing nicely. These roses grow better than the ones we purchased locally.—Anita C. Aurelio, Binalbagau, Negros, P. I.

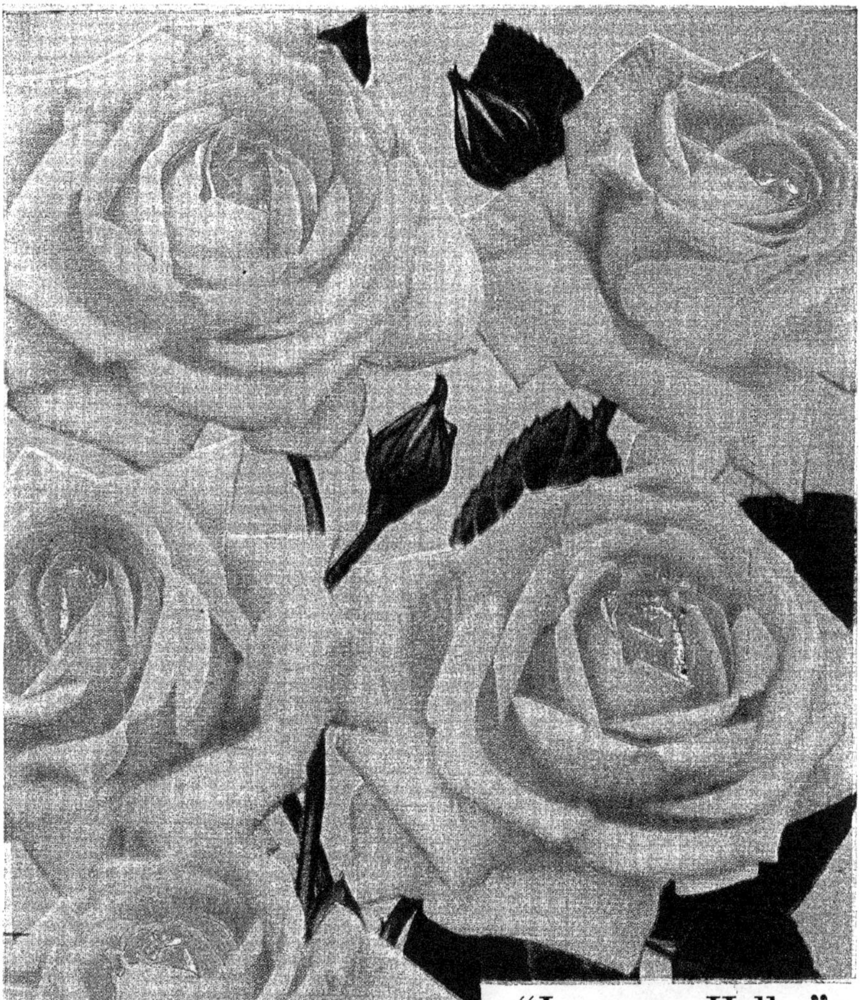

"Jeannette Heller"

So difficult is it to describe, let alone to illustrate, our great "Jeannette Heller" bush rose, that we wish to say the above illustration comes as near showing it in its natural colors as it is possible for the printing art to produce. There are many variations of colors that this wonderful rose shows. The above illustration gives some idea of its delicate color combinations. Hundreds of thousands of this great rose have been sold to satisfied customers all over the world. It stands out as one of the greatest of garden roses—one you simply must have.

RHODE ISLAND. I was greatly surprised and delighted with the nice large Carnation plants and they were so nicely packed.—Mrs. J. Gendron, Central Falls, R. I.

Famous Jeannette Heller Rose

Introduced and for Sale by Heller Brothers Company

THE BEST, STRONGEST, HEALTHIEST, HARDIEST AND MOST BEAUTIFUL BUSH ROSE IN THE WORLD.

Reasons Why "Jeannette Heller" is the one Best Rose for American Gardens.

Always in Bloom. The prime requisite of any rose is to bloom abundantly. "Jeannette Heller" blooms literally all the time and the first year. Here in New Castle growing in ordinary garden soil, we saw a bush about two feet high of "Jeannette Heller" with seventeen perfect flowers and buds at one time. What rose can equal that?

Healthiest of All Roses. Has wonderful vigor. The reason "Jeannette" blooms so abundantly is that it has a wonderfully strong root action, which means perfect health, as the heart of any rose is its root system. Has the vigor of an oak. Hardy with protection under ordinary conditions.

Grows Luxuriantly Everywhere. "Jeannette Heller" is not partial to any particular section of the country. It grows sturdily and beautifully everywhere. We have seen it still in bloom while covered with ice and sleet. Even in Jamaica, under the tropical sun, we saw a bush covered with a perfect mass of gorgeous buds and flowers. Splendid in the extreme cold climates, superb in the West, grows like a weed in the South, the East has pronounced it the best rose in America for amateur planters.

Perfect Flowers, Superb Color. Perfect flowers both in form and color. The flowers are magnificent, buds long and pointed, of immense size, opening into wonderful, deep, double, perfectly formed blooms, unsurpassed and indescribable in their beauty. The color is a beautiful blending of shell-pink in the center, shading off to rosy blush and pale yellow; sometimes creamy yellow and pale white or pearl, then again almost pure pink. Impossible to describe the different color effects, which are duplicated in no other rose.

A Truly American Rose. This is an American rose, born in America. It wants a permanent home in every garden in America. The best rose for amateur rose growers. Read what others have to say and what you will say about "Jeannette Heller" when you try it.

The rose plants I received from you this spring were all that could be desired, as they have grown and bloomed wonderfully. I can't say too much for the Heller Roses. Quite a few of my friends made special trips to see my roses and I have recommended them very highly to all. I can't think of any rose more beautiful than the "Jeannette Heller." Mrs. Robert Hollstander, St. Joseph, Missouri.

The "Jeannette Heller" rose is by far the most satisfactory rose I have ever seen. Mrs. G. R. McGrew, Dallas, Texas.

I already have some of your roses, among them the beautiful "Jeannette Heller." It was three years old last summer and at one time had fifty-six blooms and buds on it. Mrs. F. A. Weigel, Louisville, Kentucky.

All roses received from you are wonderful. "Jeannette Heller" sure is the "Queen of them all." Mrs. F. E. Simmons, Seattle, Wash.

PRICES. Strong, first size pot-plants, 30c each; 4 for $1.00; $2.50 per doz., postpaid by mail. Large, two year old plants with soil on roots, 90c each; $10.00 per doz., by express; $1.00 each, prepaid by parcel post. Star size, pot-grown, specimen plants, $1.25 each, by express; prepaid by parcel post, $1.50 each. ON OWN ROOTS.

NOTE: Please Keep This Book for Reference. You Will Need It.

PHILIPPINE ISLANDS. All the roses purchased from you are growing nicely. These roses grow better than the ones we purchased locally.—Anita C. Aurelio, Binalbagau, Negros, P. I.

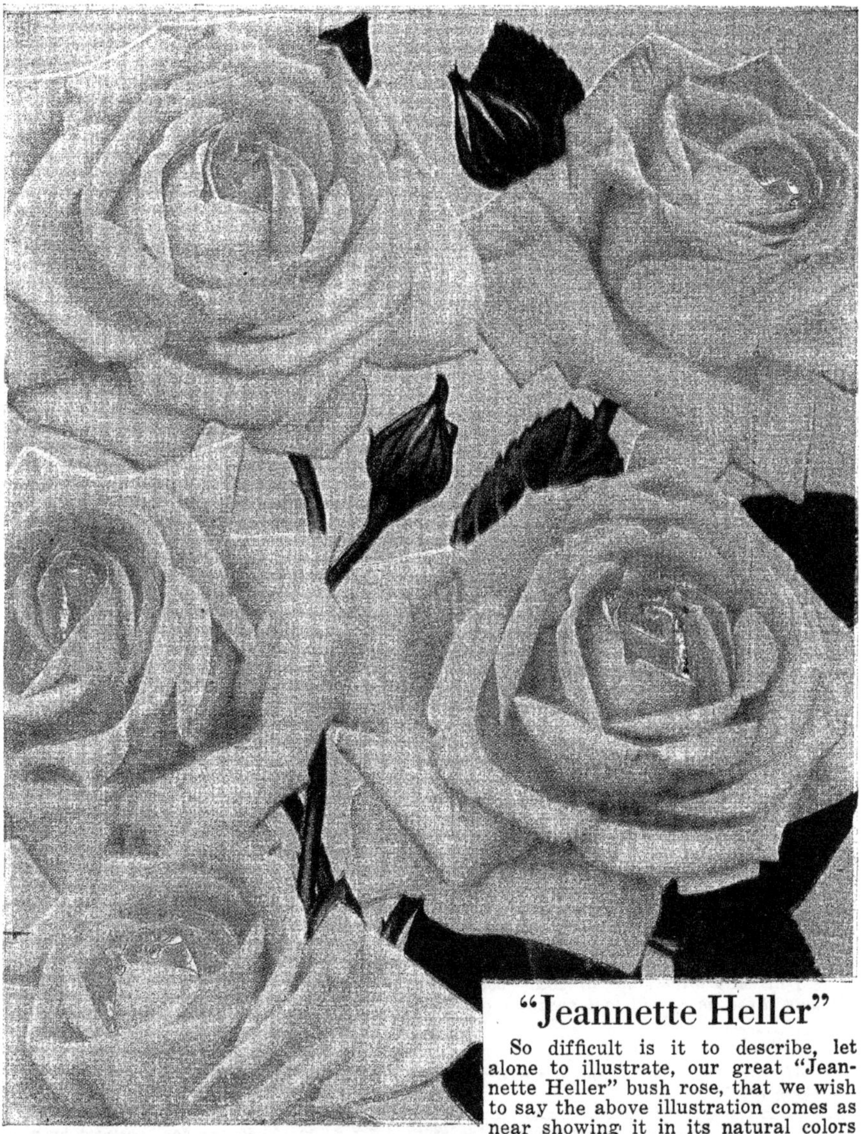

"Jeannette Heller"

So difficult is it to describe, let alone to illustrate, our great "Jeannette Heller" bush rose, that we wish to say the above illustration comes as near showing it in its natural colors as it is possible for the printing art to produce. There are many variations of colors that this wonderful rose shows. The above illustration gives some idea of its delicate color combinations. Hundreds of thousands of this great rose have been sold to satisfied customers all over the world. It stands out as one of the greatest of garden roses —one you simply must have.

RHODE ISLAND. I was greatly surprised and delighted with the nice large Carnation plants and they were so nicely packed.—Mrs. J. Gendron, Central Falls, R. I.

Famous Jeannette Heller Rose

Introduced and for Sale by Heller Brothers Company

THE BEST, STRONGEST, HEALTHIEST, HARDIEST AND MOST BEAUTIFUL BUSH ROSE IN THE WORLD.

Reasons Why "Jeannette Heller" is the one Best Rose for American Gardens.

Always in Bloom. The prime requisite of any rose is to bloom abundantly. "Jeannette Heller" blooms literally **all the time and the first year.** Here in New Castle growing in ordinary garden soil, we saw a bush about two feet high of "Jeannette Heller" with **seventeen perfect flowers and buds at one time.** What rose can equal that?

Healthiest of All Roses. Has wonderful vigor. The reason "Jeannette" blooms so abundantly is that it has a wonderfully strong root action, which means perfect health, as the heart of any rose is its root system. Has the vigor of an oak. Hardy with protection under ordinary conditions.

Grows Luxuriantly Everywhere. "Jeannette Heller" is not partial to any particular section of the country. It grows sturdily and beautifully everywhere. We have seen it still in bloom while covered with ice and sleet. Even in Jamaica, under the tropical sun, we saw a bush covered with a perfect mass of gorgeous buds and flowers. Splendid in the extreme cold climates, superb in the West, grows like a weed in the South, the East has pronounced it the best rose in America for amateur planters.

Perfect Flowers, Superb Color. Perfect flowers both in form and color. The flowers are magnificent, buds long and pointed, of immense size, opening into wonderful, deep, double, perfectly formed blooms, unsurpassed and indescribable in their beauty. The color is a beautiful blending of shell-pink in the center, shading off to rosy blush and pale yellow; sometimes creamy yellow and pale white or pearl, then again almost pure pink. Impossible to describe the different color effects, which are duplicated in no other rose.

A Truly American Rose. This is an American rose, born in America. It wants a permanent home in every garden in America. The best rose for amateur rose growers. Read what others have to say and what you will say about "Jeannette Heller" when you try it.

The rose plants I received from you this spring were all that could be desired, as they have grown and bloomed wonderfully. I can't say too much for the Heller Roses. Quite a few of my friends made special trips to see my roses and I have recommended them very highly to all. I can't think of any rose more beautiful than the "Jeannette Heller."   *Mrs. Robert Hollstander, St. Joseph, Missouri.*

The "Jeannette Heller" rose is by far the most satisfactory rose I have ever seen.   *Mrs. G. R. McGrew, Dallas, Texas.*

I already have some of your roses, among them the beautiful "Jeannette Heller." It was three years old last summer and at one time had fifty-six blooms and buds on it.   *Mrs. F. A. Weigel, Louisville, Kentucky.*

All roses received from you are wonderful. "Jeannette Heller" sure is the "Queen of them all."   *Mrs. F. E. Simmons, Seattle, Wash.*

PRICES. Strong, first size pot-plants, 30c each; 4 for $1.00; $2.50 per doz., postpaid by mail. Large, two year old plants with soil on roots, 90c each; $10.00 per doz., by express; $1.00 each, prepaid by parcel post. Star size, pot-grown, specimen plants, $1.25 each, by express; prepaid by parcel post, $1.50 each. **ON OWN ROOTS.**

NOTE: Please Keep This Book for Reference. You Will Need It.

How to Grow the "Roses of New Castle"

THE REAL TEST of a rose is in its roots. The root action is the heart of the plant. The *"ROSES OF NEW CASTLE"*, grown by skilled growers are prepared especially for the amateur planter. Before the plants are shipped the roots are developed by our own special methods and instead of expecting you to develop the roots, which you must do when you plant dormant, budded and grafted plants, without active working roots, we remove that risk, which takes practically all doubt out of rose growing. Why should you take that risk when you can secure these famous "ROSES OF NEW CASTLE", pot grown, on their OWN ROOTS at a much less price than the Nursery grown, budded, dormant, wild-root roses?

PREPARATION OF SOIL. There is no mystery connected with successful home, yard or garden rose growing. The many articles appearing in various publications, giving elaborate instructions as regards soil, drainage, a multitude of "don't and does" to follow, lists of obscure roses unsuited to American climatic conditions, all of which is discouraging and represents so much misinformation, confuses the mind of the average amateur. Rose growing is not a burden. It is one of the greatest pleasures of life. Good garden soil such as will grow corn, peas, beans, etc. is ideal. When it is possible enrich the soil with well rotted manure. Cow manure is best.

Horse manure, if thoroughly rotted, will do. Use chicken, pig, sheep and other animal manures sparingly, if at all. Bone meal, air slacked lime, Walker's Plant Food may be used lightly, very lightly. Spade deep—fifteen inches or more for reasonable drainage and to hold moisture in hot weather.

WHEN TO PLANT. Plant after all danger of frost is past, and any time thereafter that suits you. There is no closed season for planting our roses; being pot grown, they can be set out in the Northern and Middle states any time during the growing season, spring, summer and fall. In the Southern and Pacific Coast States, plant whenever it suits best. Our plants are always ready to plant and with perfect safety as they are always pot-grown.

HOW TO PLANT. Plant 18 to 24 inches apart as a rule but you can plant to suit your space. Put the plants well into the ground, firm thoroughly leaving a slight depression around them to hold moisture. After planting, water the plants thoroughly until you are sure the soil at the bottom of the roots is well dampened, then do not water too much after that. Roses are like corn, they like hot dry spells and heavy rains. If possible, syringe the foliage frequently with water under pressure. As the plants bloom cut the flowers and have the pleasure out of them. As you cut them it helps to develop more blooming shoots. Do not feed the plants until they are growing actively, then feed lightly, using Walker's Plant Food or Stim-U-Plant Tablets, which we offer. For insects, if they appear, use Sulpho Tobacco Soap or Melrosine and apply with a Tyrian Plant Sprinkler or Hudson Fog Sprayer which we offer in this book.

WINTER PROTECTION. More rose plants are killed from protecting too early than all other causes combined. Do not commence protection until real freezing weather comes—then commence to put some soil up around the plants, a little at a time and as the weather gets colder put a little covering of leaves, straw, litter, allowing for circulation of air. Do not smother the plants out. In the spring remove the covering gradually as it was put on. The greatest value of the "ROSES OF NEW CASTLE" for the amateur is they are on their OWN ROOTS and if the tops are completely killed back and any part of the root still lives you still have a growing plant. Don't protect too early and

2 year old Rose plant taken out of the pot. Showing how the soil remains on the roots.

don't leave the protection stay on too long in the early Spring.

6

PRUNING. When plants fail to mature the buds which they bear, pinch off some of the undeveloped buds and imperfect blooms, and feed lightly. In the early spring plants can be pruned back about one-third of their present growth, before they foliage out.

GENERAL INFORMATION. After planting, if the leaves turn yellow and drop off, do not be alarmed. Nature thus conserves the vitality of the plant. Immediately the plant will throw out new and stronger shoots. During the growing season if the plants develop diseased foliage that indicates the root action is poor and the plant needs nourishment, in the way of a good plant food. We recommend the insecticides and fertilizers listed on this page, to promote health and vigor. Roses like sunshine. Partial shade is not so harmful but they do best in full sunshine. Do not plant too close to trees or shrubs.

WRITE US IF YOU NEED HELP. Feel free to write us at any time. We will help you in every way we can. If you are in doubt about the proper selection you can safely leave it to us. If the plants do not develop as they should, write us and it is possible we can help you. With the vigor, vitality and general health of our plants, if these simple instructions are followed, it will be the exception to the rule if you do not have splendid success with our roses.

2-year-old, Pot-grown Rose plant

Insecticides and Fertilizers

WALKER'S PLANT FOOD. A highly concentrated plant food quickly producing vigorous healthy growth and profusion of flowers. Directions with each package. 2½ oz. cans, making 3 gals., postpaid 25c; 5 oz. cans, making 6 gals., postpaid 45c; 12 oz. cans, making 15 gals., postpaid 70c.

STIM-U-PLANT TABLETS. An excellent plant food in tablet form. Increases growth marvelously. Complete directions with each package. Prices, postpaid: Small size, 25c; 100 tablets, 75c; 1,000 tablets, in bucket, $3.50 postpaid.

MELROSINE. Sure remedy for all rose and other plant pests. Full directions with each package. Pint, $1.15; quart, $1.95, postpaid.

SULUPHO-TOBACCO SOAP. For sure, easy and immediate extermination of all insect life on plants, trees and animals. Sulpho-Tobacco Soap is a matchless preparation. Will not injure most tender plant. Dissolves readily in water, and may be applied with an ordinary sprayer. 3 oz. cake, 15c; 8 oz. cake, 30c, postpaid.

2-year-old Rose Plants, wrapped ready for shipment.

HOW MUCH LONGER THIS SPRING CAN YOU FILL ORDERS? This is a question frequently asked because our friends think we are Nurserymen, which are not. Nursery grown budded and grafted roses on wild roots are dormant when shipped, that is, they have no leaves on them, have been kept in cold storage through the winter, and they must be planted like a tree, early in the spring. Our rose plants **are on their own roots,** and as long as any considerable part of the roots is left you have a rose. They are grown in large pots or crocks, under glass, in Nature's own way in the sunshine, and have masses of strong, active roots and are in full foliage when shipped, ready for immediate results. They can be shipped and planted any time in the year during the growing season. There is no closed season for the Roses of New Castle, **grown in pots and on own roots.**

Rare Creations in New Garden Roses

Our offerings in new roses embrace exquisite varieties, marvelous in form, colo and fragrance. It is impossible to find space to describe them properly. They mar the scientific advancement the world over in the realm of roses. Of necessity ou supply is limited, therefore order early. They are essentially garden roses and wi do well in any climate; hardy, free blooming and superb in their wondrous beauty.

Rev. F. Page Roberts

Hybrid Tea—No rose in recent years has impressed us more than has this variety. A splendid, vigorous growing bush rose, carrying its superb, sweetly scented flowers erect on long stiff stems. As to the color it is difficult to describe, copper red going to golden yellow with the outside of petals a reddish tint—a most charming effect. Flowers very large and double, with 40 to 50 petals, and highly fragrant. A truly magnificent rose.

* Red Columbia

Hybrid Tea—Same as Columbia except the color is a brilliant scarlet crimson of exquisite shading; if anything it is freer, more constant bloomer than Columbia.

Hugonis

A rare novelty, known as the "Golden Rose of China". Very unique, blooming early in the spring before all other varieties, bearing masses of single yellow flowers. Extremely hardy. Two-year-old plants only.

Price two year old plants, only, $1.00 each by express $1.10, prepaid by parcel post.

Lord Charlemont

Hybrid Tea—Flowers clear crimson, deepening to carmine crimson with almost black shadings, perfectly shaped long pointed buds, large and full sweetly scented flowers. Free-growing and free-flowering, a splendid Rose of exceptional richness and beauty.

Matchless

Matchless

Hybrid Tea—An offspring of the Gre Premier has created a sensation in t rose world. Fully as large, if not larg than Premier. Full, deep, double. Mag ficent, long buds on long, strong ste Color deep, rosy cerise, deepening to pu red. Always in bloom. Ranks with Americ Beauty in color.

Edel

Hybrid Tea—Bud very large, flower lar double, well-built, stately; opens well all weather; sweet fragrance. Color wh with faintest ivory shading toward ba Foliage very bold and distinct. A v vigorous grower and constant bloomer.

* Red Giant

Hybrid Tea—Another very fine new b rose of strong growth, free of insects, cause of that fact; bears its lovely carm colored flowers constantly through the gr ing season. The color is new, attractive different; it is well named. You will l this splendid new rose.

Price of all roses on this page, except where ed. Strong, first size, pot plants, 35c each; 3 $1.00 postpaid; strong two-year-old pot grown pla soil on roots, $1.00 each by express; prepaid by cel post, $1.10 each; Star size plants, $1.25 by press; $1.40 each by parcel post prepaid.

Rev. F. Page Roberts

* David O. Dodd

Hybrid Tea—New American bush rose of magnificent form and color. Rich, deeply flushed crimson scarlet of flaming color, large beautifully shaped buds and enormous double flowers. Stronger growing than any crimson rose in the list. Don't miss this great rose. Deliciously fragrant.

Pink Beauty

Hybrid Tea—Strong bush type, free blooming with immense, beautifully shaped buds opening into large globular, satiny pink flowers, changing to paler pink when the bloom is fully open.

* Royal Red

Hybrid Tea—A giant bush rose with flowers of enormous size. Color magnificent scarlet red, with almost black shading in the bud and half-open flower, while the expanded flower, which is of enormous size, shows lighter in color. Sweetly scented; strong, powerful stem.

* Templar

Hybrid Tea—Clear bright red of exceedingly double form and fine, strong stems. Flowers of medium size and very globular. Few thorns and highly scented. Vigorous grower and continuous bloomer.

* Freedom

Climbing White American Beauty. Hybrid Tea. Strong grower. Variety similar to Kaiserin Augusta Victoria, but of much more vigorous growth and greater freedom of bloom. More double than Silver Moon with but one flower to the stem. A grand, new, hardy climbing rose.

Etoile de Holland

Hybrid Tea—Equisite bush rose. Color bright red, flower medium size, fairly full and deliciously perfumed. Vigorous, upright growth.

* City of Little Rock

Hybrid Tea—Beautiful in color, a bright pink. Flowers large, buds open perfectly, of ideal form. A garden bush rose, popular because of its strong vigorous growth and freedom of bloom.

* W. Freeland Kendrick

Hybrid Tea—Of the LaFrance type. Buds medium size; flowers large, globular, very double, full, lasting and fragrant; color flesh deepening to peach in center, borne singly and several together on medium length stems. Very vigorous, semi-climber and a continuous bloomer. Very hardy.

* John Cook

Hybrid Tea—Another introduction of the veteran introducer of Radiance, Francis Scott Key and many other notable varieties. Considered worthy to bear the distinguished name of the originator. An improved La France. Flowers come in clusters from two to six in great profusion; splendid in form. Color clear pink, reflex petals of a lighter shade.

Lord Lambourne

Perenetiana—Color deep yellow, each petal heavily margined carmine-scarlet—Foliage bright glossy green. Strong growing bush form. Strong fruity fragrance.

Superb New Rose, David O. Dodd

9

Sure-to-Bloom Hybrid Tea Roses

These great bush roses, which are the result of cross fertilization between the Hardy Hybrid Perpetual or June Roses and the Everblooming Tea Roses. have rapidly superseded all other classes for general planting. From June Roses they inherit the large, bold, handsome, exquisitely fragrant flowers, retaining in a marked degree their hardiness, so that they' stand the severest winters without damage, and from the Tea Roses they have retained the free and constant blooming habit. They produce their gorgeous flowers without interruption the entire growing season. Our collection includes all varieties of merit now in cultivation. All on their own roots—once planted practically permanent.

* Sensation

Well named. The sensation of the rose world. Heavy, luxuriant foliage; strong growing, magnificently formed flowers of deepest velvety crimson, massive in size produced in marvelous abundance. One of the greatest roses of recent origin.

The Great Rhea Reid

* Rhea Reid

The flowers are immense in size, full, deep and doubl They are borne in endless profusion on long, stiff erect stem The color is vivid scarlet-crimson gorgeous in appearanc

* Mad. Caroline Testout

This grand old favorite has been adopted by the State of O gon as its State Flower. In color, it is of a satiny rose, deepeni to clear red in the center.

* Francis Scott Key

A magnificent Hybrid Tea garden rose originated by the gre Rosarian, John Cook, and named in honor of the author of t "Star Spangled Banner." Color a glowing scarlet and with dar er shadings. Buds long and pointed, opening full and double.

* Amelia Gude

An offspring of Columbia with its good qualities. Flowe beautiful, of a pleasing shade of golden yellow, petals tipp with a lighter shade. Very free bloomer and a good grow Together with Columbia. Premier, Hoosier Beauty, America, M Butterfly. it represents that type of garden rose that will p many of the old favorites into discard.

Sensation

*Columbia

THE LOVELIEST PINK GARDEN BUSH ROSE

(Illustrated in Color on back cover page)

As glorious as American Beauty. A Hybrid Tea of wonderful blooming qualities, as free as any Tea Rose; blooms all the time. Almost thornless. Throws out strong, heavy shoots four feet and more in length, each producing a magnificent bloom, often measuring six inches across. Color a deep peach pink, deepening into a glowing pink, a perfect color. The fragrance is beyond description, sweeter than American Beauty. After a thorough trial we heartily recommend it as a great outdoor rose without a peer. Hardy with light protection even in extremely cold sections. Strong grower with tremendous root action—the secret of its great vigor and blooming capacity.

> *"Columbia is a most glorious rose. It produced seven blooms and is still blooming. They are simply gorgeous."* —Mrs. Tom Fraziere, Paris, Illinois.

* Climbing Columbia

Identical with the great Columbia, having all the parent's desirable features—health, vigor and beauty—and in addition it is a wonderful climber, growing ten to fifteen feet in a single season. Blooming, as it does continuously, bearing blooms of immense size, often measuring six inches in diameter, this at once becomes the greatest of all pink, hardy, ever-blooming, climbing roses. Color is the same as Columbia, glowing pink; fragrance delicious. A most remarkable rose and scarce.

* Souv. Claudius Pernet

Pernetiana—Supreme yellow, rose strong growing bush, magnificent foliage. Perfectly formed flowers. Absolutely new in color—deep lemon yellow without spot or blemish. Wonderfully free blooming.

Two year old plants only, price $1.00 each, by express; $1.10 prepaid by parcel post.

Columbia (Pink)

Los Angeles

Pernetiana—Growth vigorous, producing in continued succession during growing season, strong shoots, each one bearing an enormous flower of a luminous flame pink, toned with coral and shaded with translucent gold at the base of petals.

Two year old plants only, price $1.00 each by express, $1.10 prepaid by parcel post.

Price of all roses on this page, except where noted: Strong, first size, pot grown plants, 30c each; strong, two-year-old pot grown plants, soil on roots, $1.00 each by express; prepaid by parcel post, $1.15 each. Star size plants, $1.25 by express; $1.40 prepaid by parcel post.

CUSTOMERS THE WORLD OVER

It is almost a daily occurence for us to ship goods to all parts of the civilized world. The following unsolicited testimonials will convince you that no matter where you live we ship our goods safely everywhere. The skill of our packing department enables us to guarantee safe arrival of all our goods anywhere in the United States. No matter where you live in the U. S. proper you are just the same as our next door neighbor.

Grand Palace, Bangkok, Siam.

"I beg to acknowledge receipt of the roses, phlox, etc. I am very glad to say that all are O. K. Only three plants were a little wilted." Phra Khun Byubatwa.

Nassau, Bahamas

"The Columbia rose plants I ordered came the long distance as though you had passed them over the fence. Already I have had some wonderful blooms." W. W. Antonio.

Congo Belge, S. W. Africa.

"Roses sent me were just a day short of two months en route. I am delighted to report they are growing fine." Dr. Catharine Mabie.

Belize, British Hunduras.

"I received the plants and they are all in fine condition."—Denbigh Jeffery.

These are just a few tstimonials taken at random from satisfied customers. We have thousands of them from every state and every nation of the earth.

* Pink Radiance

An American Triumph. Not to be out-done by European growers. Charming in every particular, gloriously formed flowers, immense in size, exquisite fragrance, grand foliage, healthy growing, fine color and freedom of bloom. In color of flower it is both unique and beautiful—a bright carmine-rose with opal and coppery reflections. Hardy everywhere with protection; as its name suggests, is radiantly beautiful.

Madam Butterfly

When its merits become known this great variety will probably be the most popular rose in cultivation. To describe this rose is impossible. If you can, imagine exquisitely formed buds of Indian ochre with yellow at the base and those intermediate tones of clear, brilliant shades of coral pink, opening into deep, full flowers. Add to this delicious fragrance, and what more might be asked of a rose?

Pink Radiance

* Jonkheer J. L. Mock

Gigantic flowers on erect, stiff stems and a growth that is marvelous in its freedom. Large, heavy foliage; quickly makes a great strong bush. Flowers, enormous in size, magnificently formed, deep and double, color bright, rich pink, faced with carmine. A wonderful hardy garden rose.

* Red Letter Day

A velvety brilliant glowing scarlet-crimson bud opening into cactus-like flower which retains its color, owing to the reflex of the petals being satiny crimson scarlet, producing a rose of exquisite grace and charm.

KANSAS. The roses we had from you last year were just wonderful. They bloomed all summer and we had roses in the house the whole season.—E. N. Martin, Clay Center, Kansas.

*Kaiserin Augusta Victoria

The greatest hardy, white Hybrid Tea rose inexistence. A strong sturdy grower; free flowering; it has become the most popular of all white roses for general planting. Continuously from early spring until late fall, with pointed buds, the large, double flowers are glorious in their perfection; borne on long stiff stems; deliciously fragrant. Unexcelled for cutting. Very hardy.

Mrs. A. R. Waddell

Its beauty is beyond description. Buds and flowers immense in size, full double and beautifully made, grows sturdy and erect in the most vigorous fashion, requiring no petting and coaxing; flowers color rosy scarlet, shaded with salmon; beautiful, effective and hardy.

* Silver Columbia

An offspring of the great "Columbia," with which it is identical. The magnificent flowers, if anything, are borne in greater profusion. The fragrance is even sweeter than that found in American Beauty. Color a deep silvery pink, deepening towards the center. A remarkably strong grower.

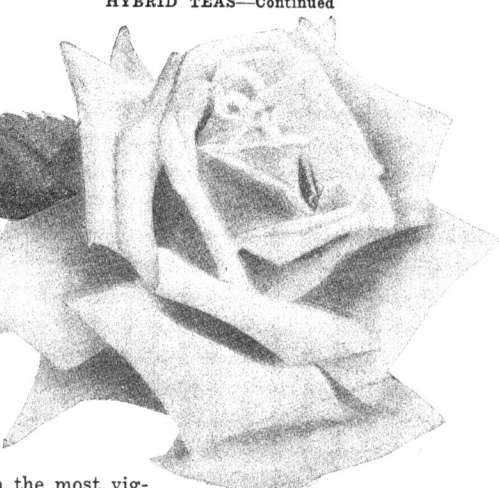

Kaiserin Augusta Victoria

* Red Radiance

A Great American Bush Rose

This great American rose is conceded by amateur and professional growers to be the best all-around garden bush rose of its color now known. Originated in America for American gardens. It has no superiors and few equals; identical with the original Radiance (pink) offered elsewhere, except the color is a splendid, even shade of clear red, without a trace of any other color, retaining its vividness for an unusually long time after being cut. The vigor of growth, its adaptability to any soil or climate has made this rose outstanding. It does just as well in the far North as in the extreme South. It is one of the twelve best garden roses in the world. Very hardy, withstanding the most severe winters. Especially recommended for its free blooming qualities in all climates.

*Helena Cambier

Of unusual beauty. Large, double, beautifully formed flowers. The colors vary from salmon rose to coppery rose. Hardy everywhere. Don't overlook this great rose.

Red Radiance

Price of all roses on this page: First size plants 30c each, any 4 for $1.00, postpaid; strong, two-year-old plants, 85c each; $9.00 per dozen assorted, by express; prepaid by parcel post 95c each. Varieties marked * can be furnished in star size or specimen plants at $1.00 each, by express; prepaid by parcel post, $1.15 each.

Lovely Killarney Roses

Pink Killarney

Yellow Killarney

This, the original introduction, is a beau_ tiful Hybrid Tea Bush Rose; strong, sturdy and upright, with fine, heavy, insect-proof fo_ liage, bearing flowers that are simply exquis_ ite in form and color; the bud is exceedingly long and the flowers immense in size; color deep, brilliant, sparkling shell-pink; hardy everywhere. The bush is magnificent in growth, of good size and bears its beautiful burden of flowers constantly all summer.

White Killarney

Identical with the parent variety, Pink Kil_ larney, of which it is an offspring, except in color, which is glistening white. Like Pink Killarney, its great charm lies in the beautiful shape of its buds, so distinctive that everyone recognizes it is a Killarney by its shape.

* Yellow Killarney

MME. JENNY GILLEMONT—A brilliant saffron-yellow rose, opening canary with dark golden shades. The buds are long and pointed, beautiful in form and color, the flowers are large, with immense petals. Hardy and vigorous, it is in constant bloom all summer. For the amateur this is by far a better rose than Souv. de C. Pernet, Duchess of Wellington or any other yellow rose of this type and class.

One each of the three Killarneys in first size plants sent postpaid for 85c. One each in two-year-old plants by ex- press, for $2.50, $2.75 by parcel post prepaid.

* America

This new Indiana rose a Hybrid Tea, is a most beautiful garden rose. Immense buds, long and pointed of great substance opening into enor- mous double flowers on sturdy long stems, almost thornless. Color a rose pink of peachblow shade; deli- ciously fragrant; every shoot pro- duces a flower. Well worthy of the name it bears.

Price of all roses on this page: Strong, first size pot-plants, 30c each, any four for $1.00, postpaid; extra heavy, two-year-old plants, with soil on roots, 85c each, $9.00 per dozen assorted, by express by parcel post, 95c each. Varieties marked * can be furnished in star or specimen plants at $1.10 each, by express; prepaid by parcel post, $1.30 each.

Pink Killarney

*Premier a Wonderful Garden Rose

The blooms are immense, often measuring 5 and 6 inches across the open flower; buds long, full pointed. Color rich, deep, rose-pink, without shadings, which is retained well, except in excessive heat. Growth is sometimes slow in getting started, but then it is very vigorous. This rose is a profuse bloomer, and the beauty of its blooms is seldom equalled. No rose garden is complete without it.

Hoosier Beauty

No illustration, no description can give the faintest idea of the grandeur of this variety. It is exquisitely beautiful, wonderfully strong growing, bushy form, producing its gorgeous flowers in the utmost profusion all the time—a single plant will give an abundance of magnificent blooms this year. And such flowers. Deep, double, immense in size, gloriously formed, with a color seen in no other rose, a superb velvety crimson. A splendid garden rose.

Price of all roses on this page: Strong, first size pot-plants, 30c each, any 4 for $1.00 postpaid; extra heavy, two-year-old plants, with soil on roots, 85c each, $9.00 per dozen assorted, by express; prepaid by parcel post, 95c each. Varieties marked * can be furnished in star size or specimen plants at $1.00 each, by express; prepaid by parcel post, $1.15 each.

Marvelous Premier

* Sunburst
Giant Yellow

Strong growing yellow roses are scarce. This gorgeous variety is the finest of all yellow roses in commerce, and in its color equal to an American Beauty or Killarney. Immense buds, long and pointed on strong stout stems opening into beautiful gigantic, full, deep, double flowers which are borne continuously. Color coppery yellow, with golden orange in deeper shades. Entirely distinct. Magnificent bush rose, stands four feet or more in height. Foliage immense in size and strong, vigorous in habit of growth. Superb. Excellent for growing in pots as well as for out door culture.

Glorious Sunburst

15

HYBRID TEAS—CON'T.

* Courtney Page

Fine habit of growth. Magnificent flowers which attract more attention from visitors than any other rose in our collection. Large, beautifully formed, full, double flowers of intense glowing crimson overlaid with a velvety sheen. A wonderfully impressive rose.

* American Beauty

The fame of American Beauty roses is world wide, This magnificent rose still reigns supreme. The rich, glowing crimson flowers, shaded and veined, are immense in size. Very double. Borne on long, stiff stems and the fragrance is that of the old Damask rose. Exquisite and unequaled. Generally hardy in all sections with winter protection.

Courtney Page
A Great Bush Rose

* Kootenay

Magnificent new Hybrid Tea rose, bearing flowers immense in size, full and double of rounded form with petals of good substance. A strong, upright grower, bush type, and claimed to be an improved Ka'serin Augusta Victoria with a larger flower. Color creamy white, a decidedly valuable addition to the white section, still very rare and scarce. A very profuse bloomer, always full of buds and blooms.

* Crimson Queen

There is no color that produces the show that a good crimson does. The color is a rich, bright, velvet crimson. A strong, vigorous, upright grower; flowers large and full. It is always in bloom, extremely hardy and produces a magnificent bush in a short time.

National Emblem

Ought to be in every home. The color is unsurpassed—a crimson, overlaid with deep, velvety crimson, shading to deeper vermilion edges; buds long and pointed, blooms full, deep and double, unusually well formed for a red rose. Petals of heavy substance, making it fine for cutting as well as garden decoration. Gorgeous in their almost barbaric beauty; delicious fragrance.

* Senator Mascurand

Yellow Hybrid Tea rose, the center of a bloom resembling the color of the yolk of an egg, toning to high sulphur-yellow. Slender, tapered buds, opening into large, full, globular blooms. Very strong, healthy grower and free bloomer. Blooms of large, perfect shape. Mildly fragrant. Prefectly hardy.

Price of all roses on this page: First size plants, 30c each, any 4 for $1.00, postpaid; strong, two-year-old plants, 85c each, one or more varieties $9.00 per dozen, by express. Prepaid by parcel post, 95c each. Varieties marked * can be furnished in star or specimen plants at $1.00 each, by express, or prepaid by parcel post, $1.15 each.

Kootenay

My Jeannette Heller has twelve most beautiful roses on it. It is worth many times its cost and I will tell others about mine.—Mrs. T. J. Coomes, Louisville, Ky.

* Gruss an Teplitz

The Sweetest, Richest Crimson Hybrid Tea Rose

Called by some growers Virginia R. Coxe. The intense, dazzling color of this rose is found in no other variety. Fiery crimson, shaded with a dark, velvety sheen, totally unlike any other color in the world. Large, handsome, moderately double flowers. Produced in wonderful profusion. The flowers are produced singly, sometimes in clusters, producing a gorgeous effect all summer through. A strong, vigorous grower, actually attaining a height of four to five feet, perfectly hardy everywhere.

* Prince E. C. d'Arenberg

This really great rose seems to be overlooked. Flowers of a bright scarlet, shaded maroon, borne on long, straight, upright stems. Buds are long and pointed, opening full and double. Magnificent in form. A grand grower, with good foliage. Very hardy. Be sure to try it. A real garden rose.

PLEASE NOTE—The demand for a thoroughly hardy Everblooming Climbing Rose is abundantly served in Climbing Gruss an Teplitz offered on page 21. Just the same as the bush form except it is a most vigorous climber.

Gruss an Teplitz

* Alexander Hill Gray

After a thorough trial, both indoors, under glass and in the open ground, we are convinced that this lovely yellow bush rose is one of the very best, if not the best, of its class and color. The color, which is a deep lemon-yellow, deepening as the flower expands, does not fade in the open ground. Buds and blooms are of perfect form and great substance, and produced in great abundance throughout the entire season. Strong grower and hardy.

Mrs. Aaron Ward

Very distinct, coppery orange in the bud, golden orange when partly developed, and pinkish fawn when fully opened. Flowers splendid in form, always blooming; magnificent foliage.

I have bought roses from different places. Yours have been more successful to grow than others and they are all beautiful.—Mrs. Ew. Tomppert, Louisville, Ky.

Prices of all roses on this page: **First** size plants 30c each, any 4 for $1.00, postpaid; strong, two-year-old plants, 85c each, $9.00 per dozen assorted by express; prepaid by parcel post 95c each. Varieties marked * in star size or specimen plants at $1.00 each, by express prepaid by parcel post, $1.15 each.

Alexander Hill Gray

17

Great Yellow Rose
Etoile de Lyon

Hardy Everblooming Tea Roses

To this class of bush roses belongs all honor. Of strong, healthy, hardy habit of growth, they thrive splendidly in all parts of the country, blooming continuously, and with their handsome, deliciously perfumed flowers and healthy foliage their place in American gardens is secure and everlasting. They are quite hardy, but where the winters are extremely severe, protect them carefully.

* Etoile de Lyon

Magnificent golden yellow. One of the hardiest of yellow Tea Roses. The plants make a strong, healthy growth and bear large flowers of excellent substance with astonishing freedom. The shape of the flowers is superb and in size they rival the well known Marechal Niel. This and the Alexander Hill Gray are the two great Yellow Tea Roses.

* Bridesmaid

This variety is valuable for cutting and does finely in the open ground; color fine, clear dark pink, much deeper and more constant in color than Mermet. Strong, vigorous grower, bearing its flowers on long, sturdy stems. Still holds its own as one of the most beautiful Tea bush roses.

Price of all roses on this page: Strong, first size pot-plants, 25c each, any 5 for $1.00, postpaid; extra heavy, two-year-old plants, 80c each, $8.50 per doz., assorted, by express; by parcel post prepaid, 90c each. All on own roots. Large specimen star size plants $1.00 each, by express; prepaid by parcel post, $1.15 each.

Bridesmaid (Beautiful Pink)

18

Mad. Francisca Kruger

* Mad. Francisca Kruger

This beautiful rose is of strong, bushy habit. The flowers are very large, well filled; color salmon, deeply shaded coppery yellow. Always in bloom.

* Mrs. B. R. Cant

Especially recommended for outdoor cultivation as one of the best, if not the best rose of its class and color now in cultivation. Exceedingly hardy, producing in marvelous profusion deep crimson-pink flowers with silvery rose center, perfectly double, delightfully fragrant.

* Wm. R. Smith

Especially suited for outdoor planting and cutting purposes. The soft blending of the salmon-pinks, rose pinks, and the magnificent flesh tints resemble the blush of a maiden's cheek. The flowers are large, full and double, and most exquisitely formed.

* Lady Hillingdon

Color almost beyond description, apricot-yellow, shaded to orange on the outer edge of the petals, becoming deeper and more intense toward the center of the bloom. Buds produced on long, strong wiry stems, well above the foliage, giving a graceful effect. **Strong,** healthy grower.

* Marie Guillot

The color is pure white, sometimes faintly tinged pale yellow. The flowers are beautifully made, very large, full and double, the buds are very pretty, of sweet fragrance.

* The Bride

There is no other white rose more satisfactory than the Bride. The buds and flowers are unusually large, well formed and deliciously perfumed. When planted in the open ground the flowers are sometimes found to be delicately tinted with pink, making it exceedingly attractive. Strong, healthy growth and a profuse bloomer.

* Cornelia Cook

Flowers borne in great profusion and very desirable; color pure creamy white, tinged with lemon and blush.

Lady Hillingdon

Dainty Baby Doll

"Baby Doll" Rose

EXQUISITELY BEAUTIFUL—RIVALS THE RAINBOW

Our New and Most Sensational Hardy Everblooming Bush Rose

Has taken the country by storm. The most unique rose ever introduced. The long, slender, deep green foliage is three times as plentiful as is usually found on any rose and is insect proof. It grows not to exceed 15 inches high. The smallest bush produces hundreds of perfectly formed miniature blooms, early and late, in marvelous profusion, all the time, outdoors and indoors in pots. The plant is always blooming!

For all purposes there is nothing like it anywhere; in hardiness and health it is superb. The flowers are exquisitely formed. No description can picture the daintiness and the beauty of the bloom; nothing has ever been seen like it in the rose family in the centuries gone by. The tips of the petals show vivid crimson, then that mellows down through shades of pink into saffron, lavender, gold and yellow and finally into deep old gold—a combination so extraordinary and so entrancing that immediately upon seeing the rose, the exclamation is heard, "What a wonderful rose."

Ours is the original stock introduced in America for the first time as one of the famous "Roses of New Castle." Don't miss it.

CLOTILDE SOUPERT—Hybrid Polyantha. Known the world over as one of the very best of all bedding Roses. A strong dwarf grower and a wonderful bloomer, producing clusters of the finest formed flowers. Full, double and deliciously sweet. Color effect is beautiful, ivory white, shading toward the center to silvery rose.

GRUSS AN AACHEN—A Hybrid Polyantha, but looks more like a Hybrid Tea. Low growing and sturdy, fine large foliage. Practically insect-proof. Color yellowish rose with salmon pink and rose shadings. Splendid flowers. A remarkable new rose.

PRICE—All roses on this page. Strong one-year-old plants, 30c each; 4 for $1.00; $2.50 per doz., postpaid; extra large heavy, two-year-old plants, 85c each $8.50 per doz., by express; 95c each, postpaid by parcel post. Star size, specimen plants, $1.10 each, by express; $1.20 by parcel post, prepaid.

Free Blooming Climbing Roses

These are the best of all constant blooming climbing roses. Noted for the exquisite beauty of their flowers. Including Teas, Hybrid Teas, Polyanthas, etc. Where the winters are not too severe they are perfectly hardy, but some protection is desirable. Strong growing, bearing large flowers like the choicest bush roses, they bloom all summer through.

*Climbing Gruss An Teplitz

This is an exact counterpart of the bush rose Gruss an Teplitz, but a vigorous climber, attaining a height of 10 to 15 feet in a single season. When it first blooms in the spring it is a dazzling sheet of velvety crimson. Each bloom is produced singly on long stems, the same as the bush variety so well known. Blooms throughout the growing season. One of the greatest of all climbing roses and hardy everywhere.

*Marechal Niel

The famous old favorite which grows so luxuriantly in the South. Buds and flowers superb; extra large very double, and deliciously perfumed. Deep golden yellow. Blooms with great freedom. In the North should have very careful protection during the winter.

*Mrs. Robert Peary

(Climbing Kaiserin Augusta) — Strong, rapid grower. The lovely white flowers are magnificent beyond description, buds long and pointed.

*CLIMBING CECILE BRUNNER—Color rosy pink, rich creamy white ground. Needs protection.

*CLIMBING WHITE MAMAN CO-CHET—The exquisite white flowers are borne in great profusion. Absolutely hardy, except in the extreme North, where it requires slight protection. It is a strong, vigorous grower, throwing up strong canes 15 to 20 feet long in a single season.

*CLIMBING PINK KILLARNEY—Immense, long pointed buds with massive petals, opening into flowers of enormous size; color deep pink, deliciously fragrant.

*CLIMBING PINK MAMAN COCHET—An exact climbing counterpart of the bush variety. As free blooming as the Cochets. Will withstand the rigor of the Northern winters with protection. Superb pink flowers.

THE CHEROKEE ROSE—The bushes bear large pure white roses in great profusion. Moderately hardy.

Climbing Gruss an Teplitz

*FORTUNE'S DOUBLE YELLOW—Bronzed yellow or coppery and fawn color. (Beauty of Glazenwood.)

CLIMBING HELEN GOULD—Climbing type of the beautiful Helen Gould. Immense flowers, full and double, constantly produced. Warm watermelon-red Superior.

*CLIMBING RHEA REID—Same as Rhea Reid except of a strong climbing habit, bearing rich, deep crimson flowers constantly throughout the growing season.

*CLIMBING CLOTHILDE SOUPERT—One of the best, bearing immense clusters of flowers constantly. Ivory white shaded in center silvery pink flowers. Not excelled by any climber. Hardy.

Price of all roses on this page: Strong, first size plants, 25c each, any 5 for $1.00, postpaid; strong, two-year-old plants, 80c each; $8.50 per dozen assorted, by express; prepaid by parcel post, 90c each. Varieties marked * can be furnished in star or specimen plants at $1.00 each; by express; prepaid by parcel post, $1.15 each.

New Castle Hardy Climbing Roses

These are the roses so necessary for the home, giving it, no matter how humble or pretentious, a touch of beauty not to be had by any other form of adornment. They also have a most useful side, in that they give most delightful and refreshing shade when used on the porch, veranda or pergola. They are used very extensively in covering unsightly spots in the ground, for screening out-buildings. Are especially recommended for trailing down over embankments and for cemetery planting; not subject to insect attack. All are hardy everywhere.

*Tausendschon or Thousand Beauties

Sensational new climbing rose, producing on the same bush many different colored flowers, hence the fitting name, "Thousand Beauties." Blooming profusely from the beginning of June until the last of July; the double flowers appear in large clusters. The colors run from delicate balsam or tender rose through the intermediate shades of bright rose and carmine, with white and yellow tints showing. (See illustration.)

*PINK TAUSENDSCHON (Rosarie)—This is a bright pink form of the famous Tausendschon. A grand addition to this class.

Tausendschon

*Excelsa

The flowers are very double, produced in immense trusses of thirty to forty flowers to each truss. Color intense crimson—new and distinct. One of the great hardy climbing roses. Hardy as an oak. Lasts a life time. A gorgeous sight when in bloom.

* Dorothy Perkins

Shell-pink; extremely hardy, vigorous and free blooming. The shoots frequently grow ten to fifteen feet in one season. The flowers are borne in immense clusters of thirty or forty. They are perfectly double, and excellently adapted for cutting and decorating.

* Gardenia

(Hardy Marechal Niel)—Very fragrant; creamy yellow.

* White Dorothy Perkins

It is a rampant grower, and in a short time will cover a large trellis. The flowers are of a brilliant glistening white.

Price of all roses on this page: Strong, first size plants, 25c each, any 5 for $1.00, postpaid; extra heavy, two-year-old plants, 80c each; $8.50 per dozen assorted; prepaid by parcel post, 90c each; still larger plants, marked * in specimen or star size, $1.00 each, limited quantity, by express; prepaid by parcel post, $1.15 each. **All** on own roots.

Hardy Climbing Rose, Excelsa

* Keystone

First and Only Hardy, Free Blooming, Yellow Climbing Rose

Our illustration above gives only a faint idea of this magnificent, hardy, free-blooming yellow rose. The flowers are of fine size and wondrous beauty, borne in magnificent clusters. It has been thoroughly tested and has proved to be absolutely the finest hardy yellow rose offered. It grows more freely than any other climbing rose, is perfectly hardy even in the far North, blooms in wonderful profusion, and is absolutely immune from insect attacks and has a vigor of constitution found only in the hardy Hybrid Perpetuals.

*AUNT HARRIET—In full bloom, it is amazingly fine with its masses of dazzling scarlet-crimson roses loading every branch. The bright effect is intensified by the pure white centers and brilliant golden anthers which shine out when flowers are fully open.

*BESS LOVETT—Flowers clear bright red, good size, double, cupped form. Fragrant.

*DR. W. VAN FLEET—A splendid hardy rose, large flowers about 4 inches across, full and cup shaped; color flesh pink deepening to rosy-flesh in center.

*SILVER MOON—Blooms very large, four or more inches in diameter, pure white in color and of good substance, beautifully cupped, forming a clematis-like flower.

*MARY LOVETT—Has been termed the White Dr. Van Fleet. Hardy as an oak, a good grower, splendid for cemetery planting or wherever an absolutely hardy, white climbing rose is wanted.

*AMERICAN PILLAR—Of extremely vigorous habit of growth, the bushes being clothed in lively green from earliest spring until late in the fall. It has a profusion of bright pink, semi-double flowers in clusters which are followed by large clusters of attractive red berries.

*MARY WALLACE — Large semi-double flowers, 4 inches across; color clear rose pink with salmon at base of petals. Hardy everywhere.

EUGENE JACQUET—Immense trusses of fragrant cherry-red flowers in the greatest profusion.

EMILY GRAY—A new yellow. Glossy foliage buds long, flowers golden yellow, semi-double. Needs protection north of Washington, D. C.

*ALBERIC BARBIER—Entirely free from insect attacks; heavy waxy foliage, shines as if varnished. The beautiful yellow flowers are unusually full and double, sometimes singly, sometimes in clusters.

*CHRISTINE WRIGHT—Large, thick, leathery foliage. Flowers 4 inches in diameter: color bright, clear pink; almost double; borne in large clusters.

Price of all roses on this page: Strong, first size plants, 25c each; any 5 for $1.00, postpaid, strong, two-year-old plants, 80c each, $8.50 per doz., assorted, by express; by parcel post prepaid, 90c each; still larger plants, all varieties in star or specimen sizes, $1.00 by express; $1.15 by mail.

*The Great Climbing American Beauty Rose

A MOST SENSATIONAL NEW ARRIVAL AMONG "THE ROSES OF NEW CASTLE"

Climbing
American
Beauty

Perfect grower, wonderfully hardy and remarkably free blooming. Here we have the latest triumph in American rose growing, the true Climbing American Beauty in all its promise and glory, the realized dream of every rose grower. Almost the same as American Beauty, with smaller flowers. Medium sized flowers, each produced on separate stems in clusters, vivid rosy-crimson in color, with delicious fragrance. Borne in greatest profusion for weeks. Foliage tough and leathery, deep, glossy green, sun and insect proof. The youngest plants attain a height of 10 to 15 feet in a single season. Hardy and as sturdy as an oak in all localities. For single specimens, trailing over verandas, for trellises, anywhere and everywhere, this rose will give the greatest satisfaction. Once planted will last a lifetime.

Ours is the genuine stock. Absolutely true to name, on its own roots.

* Birdie Blye

One of the freest blooming, perfectly hardy climbers. Bushes here bloom five and six times each season; good, strong grower; foliage bright, glossy green, free from insects or disease. Blooms full and double, bright carmine, changing to bright satiny rose, very fragrant.

Birdie Blye

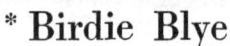

Price of all Roses on this page: Strong, first size pot-plants, 25c each, any 5 for $1.00, postpaid; extra heavy two-year-old plants, 80c each; $8.50 per doz., assorted, by express; prepaid by parcel post 90c each; larger plants marked * in specimen or star size, $1.00 each by express. Prepaid by parcel post, $1.15 each.

24

SPECIAL BARGAIN SECTION

Marvelous Bargains in Roses, Mums, Cannas, Carnations, Geraniums, Ferns, Iris, Gladioli, Etc. All Prices of Collections Offered in this Bargain Section Include Shipping Charges Prepaid to Your Door.

Out of our immense stock of Roses and other plants, for your convenience we have made up in popular priced collections, The Best both as to kinds and quality of stock. Everything the highest grade at Genuine Bargain Prices. Satisfaction and Safe Arrival is Guaranteed Anywhere in the U. S. Proper. All prices of Collections Offered in this Bargain Section Include Shipping Charges Prepaid to Your Door. All stock offered in these collections is from our regular stock of high grade plants.

"Jeannette Heller Collection of Roses"

10 WONDERFUL HELLER ROSES POSTPAID FOR $2.00

Every year we receive hundreds of letters asking us to name a collection of roses. In our vast collection the ten varieties named below are, in our opinion, among the best garden roses for all sections of the country. In this collection we include our magnificent "Jeannette Heller," the one best garden rose for American gardens.

The Famous Jeannette Heller Bush Rose

JEANNETTE HELLER— An exquisite blending of pink and cream color. Extra strong, hardy and vigorous.

BABY DOLL—The most sensational Rose; dainty, perfect flowers, colors ranging from vivid crimson to old gold; always in bloom.

CLOTHILDE SOUPERT—Color effect is beautiful, ivory-white, shading toward the center to silvery-rose.

GRUSS AN TEPLITZ—One of the most brilliant of all deep crimson garden roses.

KAISERIN AUGUSTA VICTORIA—The handsomest of all cream white roses. Very hardy and constantly in bloom.

ETOILE DE LYON — Strong-growing, healthy and wonderfully free blooming. Magnificent golden yellow.

PRINCE E. C. d'ARENBERG—Vigorous as an oak. Superbly formed flowers, bright scarlet, shaded maroon; always in bloom.

BRIDESMAID—A most beautiful, fragrant pink rose. A splendid grower. Massive flowers on long, stiff, heavy shoots. Color brilliant, sparkling shell pink. Superb.

AUNT HARRIET—New Hardy Climbing Rose. Amazingly fine with its masses of dazzling scarlet-crimson Roses loading every branch. The bright effect is intensified by the pure white centers and golden anthers.

MAD. FRANCISCA KRUGER—Strong, bushy habit. The flowers are very large, well filled; color salmon, deeply shaded coppery yellow. Always in bloom.

SPECIAL OFFER

One each, strong, vigorous, first size plants of the 10 superb roses offered above, postpaid, for $2.00. The complete set in strong, two-year old plants, on own roots, 10 in all, $7.50, by parcel post. The 10 varieties in lusty, star size plants, $12.00, Prepaid by Parcel Post.

Order as "Jeannette Heller Collection"

Grand "Surprise Collection"

12 Magnificent Two-Year Old Roses for $6.50 Postpaid

This collection is properly named. You will find it the greatest surprise you have ever had in your life. Just think of buying 12 strong, sturdy two year old roses and having them sent postpaid to your door with safe arrival guaranteed anywhere in the U. S. for the sum of $6.50! Here is the reason for this great offer. We are required to carry an immense stock and rather than carry over a surplus we make this offer to give room for new stock coming on. These are all high grade roses, many of them new and rare kinds, selling at the highest price because they are rare. We have to keep turning the stock over each year, hence this great offer which never fails of a tremendous sale. The value is so great and the price so low that it gives you a rare opportunity to secure these gorgeous rose plants not only at wholesale prices but much below the cost of production. THE SELECTION IS OURS but each plant is labeled. Don't miss this offer. Satisfied customers everywhere can testify as to this marvelous bargain.

Prince E. C. d'Arenberg

In each case the selection is ours but we will include in the "Surprise Collection" one "Mrs. B. R. Cant", the freest blooming dazzling crimson pink garden bush rose now known; "Jeannette Heller," our own rose, pink and white, the most beautiful bush rose in the world, described and illustrated elsewhere. Finally the great new rose, "Prince E. C. d'Arenberg, an imposing bright scarlet bush rose, continuous blooming, magnificent flowers and in a class by itself. The other varieties are **Our Selection** but equally valuable. You will never have an opportunity to secure such desirable rose bushes at such a price and we urge that you take advantage of this offer of 12 Strong two-year old rose plants prepaid in the U. S. for $6.50. The greatest bargain in the rose world and unequalled anywhere.

PLEASE ORDER AS "SURPRISE COLLECTION"

Great "Trial" Collection

8 Roses For $1

STRONG, HARDY, EVER-BLOOMING ROSE PLANTS

Keystone

The amazing value offered in this $1.00 "TRIAL COLLECTION" has made the greatest sale of rose plants in all history—over 80,000 collections sold to date! This great sale is conclusive proof of the wonderful merit of this introductory offer. Our magnificent collection of OWN-ROOT rose plants includes the finest varieties now known. Many superb kinds, practically unknown find prominence in this "TRIAL COLLECTION" which includes roses of all tints and shades; strong, sturdy stock, OUR SELECTION, 8 first size plants in all, each one labeled, postpaid by parcel post, safe arrival guaranteed anywhere in the U. S.—all for $1.00—or 12½c each! Immense production alone makes this marvelous offer possible. Don't miss ordering it, you will be richly repaid.

INCLUDED IN THE "TRIAL COLLECTION"

8 rose plants for $1.00, is our dainty, world famous "BABY DOLL", a "New Castle" rose, exquisitely beautiful—its many colors rival the rainbow; never out of bloom, grows only 15 inches high, equally good for garden or pot culture. We also include "Alexander Hill Gray," greatest yellow, everblooming, garden bush rose, also "Keystone," the only free blooming, hardy, yellow climbing rose. These roses alone are worth the price of the entire collection.

Please Order as "Trial Collection"

Baby Doll

'Hoosier' Collection Garden Roses

Cream of our stock, Ten for $2.00 Postpaid

Here is another collection of TEN Superb Garden Bush Roses. This selection is unsurpassed in hardiness, healthy growth, freedom of bloom and beauty of flowers. Any size will bloom constantly this year. The greatest garden roses in the world are in this collection. The price is so low as to meet the requirements of every purse. Each variety labeled. Safe arrival guaranteed anywhere in the U. S.

HOOSIER BEAUTY—The most beautiful crimson bush rose now known. Flowers deep, double, immense in size, of a velvety crimson color.

ALEXANDER HILL GRAY—The supreme yellow garden rose. The best of its class and color. Magnificent flowers, deep lemon yellow. Buds and blooms of perfect formation produced in greatest abundance. A Gold Medal variety.

PINK COCHET—The great pink garden rose. Flowers immense, perfectly double, always in bloom. The buds are large, full and firm, elegantly pointed.

BABY DOLL—The most sensational Rose; dainty, perfect flowers, colors ranging from vivid crimson to old gold; a combination unique and pleasing; always in bloom.

PREMIER—A wonderful Hybrid Tea Rose. Deep rose pink, perfect form, delicate fragrance, long stiff stems and continuously blooming.

MRS. B. R. CANT—One of the best if not the best everblooming bush Rose of its color. Strong growing, hardy. Produces during the season hundreds of deep crimson-pink flowers, rose center.

WHITE MAMAN COCHET—Superb flowers, snow white, with sometimes a faint tinge of blush. Wonderful garden rose, vigorous as an oak and hardy everywhere.

MME. JENNY GILLEMONT—A brilliant saffron-yellow rose, opening canary with dark golden shades. The buds are long and pointed, beautiful in form and color. A vigorous plant with foliage of the best type.

JEANNETTE HELLER—One of the greatest garden roses in the world, exquisite blending of pink and lighter shades. Always in bloom.

KOOTENAY — Color creamy white. Flowers immense in size. Very rare.

Hoosier Beauty

SPECIAL OFFER

This entire collection of ten magnificent Heller Roses, strong, first size plants for $2.00, postpaid by mail; the entire set, extra heavy 2-year-old plants, soil on roots, by parcel post, all charges paid, for $7.50; ten entire set of ten varieties in immense Star size plants, prepaid by parcel post for $12.00. All on their own roots, now growing in large pots or crocks, ready to produce immediate results.

Order as "Hoosier Collection."

Red Maman Cochet (Helen Gould)

White Maman Cochet

Pink Maman Cochet

Superb Hardy Cochet Roses

The Cochet roses are among the greatest of all hardy everblooming bush garden roses. No matter where you live, they are hardy, with protection, thriving vigorously and blooming with the utmost lavishness all summer through, making strong, sturdy bushes that last for years. The flowers are superb. The Cochet roses, because of their wonderful merit, are a specialty with us. Among the greatest of all garden roses and the best sellers.

*PINK MAMAN COCHET—Its large, full and firm buds show wonderful depth and richness of color as they open into very large, perfectly double flowers of splendid substance on long, stiff stems. A clear, rich pink, changing to silvery rose. Has many rivals but no superiors.

*CRIMSON MAMAN COCHET—This is one of the sweetest and best hardy Hybrid Tea Roses of its class and color. The plant grows to a strong, sturdy bush, and bears immense quantities of handsomely formed, deep, velvety crimson Roses of exquisite fragrance.

*WHITE MAMAN COCHET—In shape and size like its parent, the Pink Cochet, but of a snowy white, occasionally tinged with a pale blush. One of the finest white Roses for open-ground culture.

*RED MAMAN COCHET—A great red Rose and produces magnificent flowers in wonderful profusion on long, strong stems. Flowers are very full and of splendid substance; in color a warm crimson.

*YELLOW MAMAN COCHET—In shape, size and substance this is a typical Cochet Rose except that it is of a deep, golden yellow. It has long been considered one of the very finest yellow Roses.

First size, magnificent plants of any of the Cochet Roses, 25c each, any 5 for $1.00, postpaid; extra heavy, two-year-old plants, 85c each, $9.00 per dozen, by express; prepaid by parcel post 95c each. The demand for these wonderful Cochet Roses is enormous. Varieties marked * can be furnished in star or specimen plants at $1.25 each, by express; prepaid by parcel post $1.40 each.

SPECIAL OFFER

One each, 5 in all, of this famous Cochet Rose set, first size plants, $1.00, postpaid; the entire collection, 5 in all, in large, two-year-old plants, $4.00, prepaid by parcel post.

What 50 Cents Will Buy

Greatest Value for the Money Ever Offered
We Send out only the Highest Grade in Every Collection

The following wonderful low-priced Collections (50 cents each) are made up and offered to our friends for the purpose of having them enjoy the pleasure of growing some of the remarkable Roses and other plants we are producing. The plants and bulbs in these collections are not cheap stock, except in price—the quality is the same as that of all the stock sent out by us, and each collection is sent with our usual guarantee that they shall reach you safely anywhere in the U. S. A. proper. Sent by parcel post, postage paid. Don't fail to include some of these great bargains in your order.

PLEASE ORDER BY COLLECTION NUMBER

50c buys four splendid new hardy Tea Roses. A choice selection of colors. **No. 15**

50c buys five Elegant Chrysanthemums. The blooms, large and handsome. **No. 20**

50c buys 1 Asparagus Sprengeri, 1 Asparagus Plumosus, 1 Geranium, 1 Fern. **No. 25**

50c buys 3 hardy Hybrid Tea Roses. Beautiful colors and tints that will please. **No. 16**

50c buys four extra fine Carnation plants that will bloom for you all the season. **No. 21**

50c buys 10 fine Tuberose bulbs, 5 Excelsior Pearl, 3 Orange flowered and 2 New Variegated Leaved varieties **No. 26**

50c buys two hardy bush Roses and 2 hardy Climbing Roses. Rare and brilliant. **No. 17**

50c buys three elegant Canna plants for outdoor planting. Assorted kinds. **No. 22**

50c buys 12 new and rare Gladioli of assorted colors. A collection of splendid value **No. 27**

50c buys 3 choice Geraniums. Wonderful selection. The lovely colors will please. **No. 18**

50c buys one Phlox, two German Iris. Assorted colors and desirable in the garden. **No. 23**

50c buys three splendid Dahlia bulbs. Mixed k i n d s. Good, strong, hardy tubers. **No. 28**

50c buys four splendid Ferns. A rare opportunity to secure Ferns for your fernery or a fine addition to your window or porch box **No. 19**

50c buys one Chrysanthemum, one Canna, one Carnation, one Fern. An extra good collection that will be a continuous pleasure **No. 24**

FREE in all orders for 4 or more of these collections we will add a vigorous plant of our own world famous Rose. Jeannette Heller, **FREE**.

EXTRA SPECIAL BARGAINS

FOR $3.00 we will send, prepaid, five choice named **Peonies**, best kinds, all labeled. Once planted last a lifetime.

FOR $1.00 we will send, prepaid, five superb named **Dahlias**, best kinds, gorgeous flowers of immense size.

FOR $1.00 we will send, prepaid, four finest varieties hardy **Phlox**. Only the best. Nothing better for permanent planting, gorgeous colors.

"Columbia Set" of Roses

5 BEAUTIFUL ROSES POSTPAID $1

COLUMBIA—Magnificent, large, full and double silvery pink flowers. Fragrant as the American Beauty.

KAISERIN AUGUSTA VICTORIA—The handsomest of all cream white Roses. Very hardy and constantly in bloom.

VICTOR—Beautiful, large full flowers of great depth and richness; produced on long, stiff stems. Fragrance enchanting; color rich, deep pink.

RED RADIANCE—Rich crimson; buds and flowers large, full and double.

ALEX. HILL GRAY—Large, finely formed flowers of canary-yellow color.

Five splendid, hardy, everblooming kinds, $1.00 prepaid by parcel post. Two-year-old pot grown plants, 5 for $4.00, postpaid.

COLUMBIA—A perfect specimen of the rose family. will grow and thrive in any climate or location where roses are cultivated. Produces a world of beautiful, fragrant flowers.

Columbia

CLIMBING COLUMBIA—The same and identical to Columbia except it is a vigorous climber. Buds and blooms of immense size, borne singly on long shoots. Color clear pink. One of the most beautiful of all everblooming climbing roses.

SPECIAL OFFER S-2

One each, great Columbia Bush Rose and Climbing Columbia, strong, first size pot plants, prepaid by parcel post, 60c; extra heavy two-year old pot plants, one each, by parcel post, prepaid, $2.25; immense star size pot plants, one each prepaid by parcel post, $2.75.

SIX CHOICE GARDEN ROSES FOR $1.00

COLUMBIA—Magnificent, large full and double silvery pink flowers. Fragrant as the American Beauty.

MARIE GUILLOT—A queen among white Roses. Large, full, finely formed flowers.

RED RADIANCE—Rich crimson; buds and flowers large, full and double.

MAD. FRANCISCA KRUGER—This beautiful rose is of strong, bushy habit. The flowers are very large, well filled; color salmon, deeply shaded coppery yellow. Always in bloom.

WHITE MAMAN COCHET—The premier white garden Rose. Absolutely none better.

ALEX. HILL GRAY—Large, finely formed flowers of canary-yellow color.

SPECIAL OFFER—One each, strong plants, 6 garden Roses described above sent postpaid, for $1.00, the six in two-year old plants, for $5.00, by parcel post prepaid with soil on roots.

PLEASE ORDER AS "GARDEN" SET.

FAVORITE COLLECTION $1.00

EIGHT CLIMBING ROSES, POSTPAID, $1.00

Nothing can take the place of Climbing Roses around the home, hence their great popularity.

Climbing over trellises, arbors and covering the veranda, they are a beautiful sight. All colors and shades. Their flowers are to be cut by the armful. All are hardy, lasting a lifetime, increasing in beauty and size year after year. For hedges and for single specimens on the lawn they can be trimmed to any size and at any time. For permanent beauty in a year or two any one of them is worth many times the price of the entire collection.

This great collection, 8 Beautiful Climbing Roses, strong first size plants all on their own roots, each one labeled, our selection, 8 of them for $1.00, postpaid anywhere in the U. S. A. proper.

PLEASE ORDER AS "THE FAVORITE COLLECTION"

HELLER BROS. CO., New Castle, Ind.

*Flaming Paul's Scarlet Climber

It is generally conceded by experts that this great new climbing rose stands out as one of the few best roses for home planting. Color vivid scarlet shaded slightly crimson, almost a flaming scarlet, a new and striking color. Makes a brilliant display for a long time in the garden. Hardy everywhere. The petals do not fade like many climbing roses, but retain their bright color, and remain in bloom for weeks. A wonderfully strong grower, quickly making an immense plant 10 to 20 feet high. When in bloom is a gorgeous sight. This rose received the gold medal and cup for the best climbing rose at the National Rose Society's exhibit. Ranks first in all tests and at every exhibit. No illustration can do it justice.

At the Rose Society's Test Garden at Arlington, D. C., conducted by and in conjunction with the Agriculture Department at Washington, where the American Rose Society held its annual meeting, the most prominent rose which attracted more attention than any other was Paul's Scarlet Climber. Two specimen's trained to trellises made a wonderful show, while two that had been kept pruned as a bush rose were magnificent specimens covered with their bright, handsome, full double blooms. At that time they had been in bloom some two weeks and were still bright in color, while many more buds had not opened.

BEST CLIMBER—This great rose is a good, strong grower and soon makes a fine display. Foliage is heavy and free from mildew and disease, as well as all insects, and remains bright when through blooming. It is truly one of the most wonderful of all garden roses.

President S. S. Pennock, of the Society of American Florists, reports the following impression from the Bagatelle Gardens, Paris, where he was one of the judges at the great rose exhibition which is held there annually:

"In the roses, **Paul's Scarlet Climber** stood out in the garden by far the best among the climbers. It had been in **bloom over two weeks, was still in fine shape and attracted the public probably** more than any **other one rose in the garden.** There were several plants of Paul's Scarlet Climber, and one group of four plants, trained up in pyramid shape, made a wonderful show. This is rather an attractive way to train Climbers, especially where they are as free bloomers as Paul's Scarlet Climber, which presented almost a solid vivid red mass."

Price of Paul's Scarlet Climber: Strong, first size plants, 25c each; 5 for $1.00, postpaid; strong two-year-old plants, 80c each; $8.50 per doz. by express; prepaid by parcel post, 90c each; still larger plants, marked *, in star or specimen size, $1.00, express; prepaid by parcel post $1.15 each. On own roots.

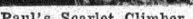
Paul's Scarlet Climber

Miscellaneous Plants for Window and Porch Boxes and Garden Bedding

Not everyone can have a flower garden but nearly every one can have a porch or window box and we list here varieties suitable for this purpose and for garden planting.

Antirrhinum

(Snap Dragon). An old favorite; has dark, glossy leaves and curiously shaped flowers with finely marked throats. Immense flowers of brilliant colors on strong stems. **Price, 10c each; 6 for 50c, postpaid.** Mixed colors.

Petunias

For freedom of bloom, variety of color and effectiveness these have no equal. They will produce their beautiful, sweet scented flowers in their delicate and gorgeous colors throughout the summer. Nothing better for window or porch boxes. We especially recommend these large flowering varieties. **CALIFORNIA GIANTS**—Immense flowers in a wide range of bright colors, beautifully ruffled and fringed. **Price 20c each; 3 for 50c, postpaid.**

Free-Blooming Fuchsias

We strongly recommend this flower for ease of culture, varied colors, profusion of bloom. Suitable alike for winter blooming or for growing outdoors either in beds or in pots or boxes as you like. The bright flowers are borne in large drooping clusters, very large and graceful. Many beautiful colors with different shadings. Mixed varieties only. **Price, 20c each; 3 for 50c postpaid.**

Geraniums

These are among the most popular of all plants for window and porch boxes and bedding. **Complete list and prices on page 36.**

Calla Lily

LILY OF THE NILE—The old favorite White Calla. Strong plants. **25c ea, postpaid.**

Calendulas

Large cut-back plants that will produce hundreds of extra large, bright orange colored flowers throughout the summer. We offer only the best and newest varieties. Fine for cutting. **Price, 15c each; $1.25 per dozen, postpaid.**

Moonflower

A handsome, quick-growing climber. Flowers 4 to 6 inches in diameter. Growth very rapid when planted in good, rich, light soil. There is no equal to it for porch and lattice.
White—Beautiful silvery white.
Blue—Same as white but color clear, satiny blue with well-defined crimson bars.
Price, 20c each; 3 for 50c, postpaid.

Kudzu Vine

Its foliage is large and bears small racemes of rosy purple, pea-shaped blossoms towards the close of August. Will grow 25 to 50 feet in one season. Splendid for covering permanently verandas, dead trees, etc. **Price, 25c each; 5 for $1.00, postpaid.**

Coleus

Plants with richly colored foliage of maroon, green, crimson, yellow, etc. Very fine for porch boxes and for pot culture. **Price 10c each; $1.00 per doz.; $7.50 per 100, ppd.**

Calla Lily

Salvia

(Scarlet Sage) Unequaled for dazzling show of fiery scarlet flowers until killed by frost. The great bedding plant. **Price, 10c each; $1.00 per dozen; $6.00 per 100, postpaid.**

Lantanas

The brilliant colors and profuse blooming habit make this a very desirable plant for porch boxes or pots or to be set out in summer. A wide range of colors. **Price, 20c each; 6 for $1.00, postpaid.**

Vinca

VARIEGATA—Beautiful trailing vine, bright green leaves bordered with creamy white. **Price, 15c each; 10 for $1.00, postpaid.**

American Wonder Lemon

Handsome, pure white flowers, nearly as large as tuberose blooms, fragrant as orange blossoms The lemons have a thin rind for such large fruit and are full of rich juice Plant in ordinary soil. in a pot or tub, and it will bear each season a fine crop. Large strong plants. **50c each, postpaid.**

Asparagus Sprengeri

For pots, vases or hanging baskets. The long, slender branches droop most gracefully. **Price, 20c each; 3 for 50c, postpaid.**

Asparagus Plumosus

Foliage resembles the finest lace. Elegant for cutting. **Price, 20c each; 3 for 50c, ppd.**

Otaheite Orange

A dwarf reproduction of the genuine fruit bearing orange tree, the flowers being identical. It flowers and fruits in pots and blooms continuously. Fragrance is delicious Fruit measures 3 ins. in diameter and is edible. Strong plants, 50c each; 5, $1.00, ppd.

Heller Chrysanthemum from a recent photo

Chrysanthemums
"Supreme Collection"
Eight Magnificent Varieties 75c

Chrysanthemums are among the most popular of all flowers for the garden. They may be termed practically hardy, as they withstand the severest winters. Flowers magnificent in form and size. They bloom in Autumn when all other flowers are gone.

Harvard—Magnificent deep crimson.
Mrs. Buckingham—Single, rosy pink.
Diana—The best pure white; late.
Yellow Bonaffon—Beautiful in form; bright yellow, standard of its color.
Chas. Rager—Large, incurved, white.
Unake — Grand incurved, beautiful lavender-pink.
Golden Glory—Bright golden yellow, immense, perfect flowers; superb.
Pacific Supreme—Pink large.

SPECIAL OFFER—One each of the eight magnificent "Mums" described above, prepaid, for 75c.

☞**PLEASE ORDER AS "SUPREME COLLECTION"**

"Pompon" Set of "Mums"

Extremely hardy, each plant producing hundreds of miniature perfectly double flowers. Show, in the extreme. Excellent for cutting. Last until frost cuts them down.
Klondike—Gorgeous bronze-yellow.   **Mrs. Buckingham**—Single rosy pink.
Golden Feather—Beautiful Golden yellow.   **Diana**—The best pure white.
L. Doty—Shell pink.
SPECIAL OFFER—One each of the above five Pompon "Mums" for 50c prepaid.
☞**PLEASE ORDER AS "POMPON SET"**

Hints on Growing Chrysanthemums

Chrysanthemums are of a very hardy nature, and may be set out from early spring clear up until cold weather. This applies to the colder sections of the country. In temperate climates, they may be planted at any time.

Plant in good rich garden soil, and do not over water but keep them moist to the bottom of the roots. Give good drainage by digging the soil deep. After the plants develop, enrich them with a good standard fertilizer such as Walker's Plant Food, Vigoro or Stim-u-Plant Tablets offered elsewhere in this book; also mulch around the plants with well rotted manure.

When flower buds appear, give them plenty of food. If you want extra large flowers, pinch off small buds leaving the strength go into the remaining ones.

For insects use Sulpho-Tobacco Soap, offered elsewhere in this book spraying the plants with this solution.

Mulch heavily during the winter. In extremely cold climates the clumps may be brought in and stored over the winter in a cool, dark cellar, then plant them out again early in Spring.

Mrs. Buckingham Pompon from a photo

Gorgeous Dahlias

No other word but GORGEOUS can describe the beauty of the Dahlias offered on this page. In the brilliant and almost barbaric combination of colors, the Dahlia has no rival. There seems to be no end to the range of color. Easy to grow, they are an immensely popular flowering plant for the garden. Plant as soon as all danger of frost is past in average garden soil; cover the tubers or bulbs about six inches deep. Cultivate well until blooms begin to show, then mulch with well rotted manure, or feed a good standard plant food, and you will be astounded with the magnificent flowers produced. Our list includes the best and most popular varieties in cultivation, and bound to please the most exacting Dahlia grower. All prices include postage, when sent by parcel post.

New and Rare Dahlias

MRS. I DE VER WARNER—Deep mauve-pink or lavender. Long, stiff stems. One of the best decorative varieties. Fine for cutting. **$1.00 each.**

EMPEROR—Decorative type, large, a deep, velvety crimson, almost maroon. **$1.00 each.**

WASHINGTON CITY—A gigantic pure white, star-like flower, cactus type. It has a long, stiff stem and holds its flower erect. **75c each.**

BILLIONAIRE—Rich, golden yellow. Immense flowers, peony type, **$1.00 each.**

JERSEY BEAUTY—A very fine, true pink, flowers of immense size, perfect shape, produced on long straight, stiff stems; very free bloomer. A truly wonderful decorative Dahlia. **$1.50 each.**

MILLIONAIRE — Delicate lavender, with faint pink cast overshading it. One of the best known lavender-pink decorative Dahlias; an immense flower. Flowers six to nine inches in diameter. **75c each.**

BERTHA STORY—A very large flower of deep rose pink on long stem. Occasionally flowers showing white petals. Remarkably free bloomer. Decorative type **75c each.**

F. W. FELLOWS—Color a bright orange-scarlet. Produces its long narrow petaled flowers in profusion. One of the very best Cactus varieties. **75c each.**

GEORGE WALTERS—Salmon pink, with touches of yellow. Producing its blooms very freely on long stiff stems. A reliable and very popular variety. Hybrid cactus. **75c each.**

KALIF—A truly majestic flower. Color a pure glowing scarlet. Gigantic flowers are held erect on strong, stiff stems. Free bloomer. Hybrid cactus. **75c each.**

AMUN RA—One of the most sensational. Giant in size and perfect in flower. Outer petals are of a gorgeous copper and orange tones shading to gold and amber, deepening in the center to a dark reddish brown. **$1.00 each.**

DR. TEVIS — Gigantic flowers on long, erect stems. Beautiful shade of salmon-rose suffused with gold. Decorative type **75c each.**

PRIDE OF CALIFORNIA —(Decorative). Called the "American Beauty" dahlia. Huge crimson-red flowers on long strong stems **75c each.**

Dahlia "Emperor"

28

Cactus Dahlias

This class produces large, loosely formed chrysanthemum-like flowers. The long, narrow petals are variously rolled and twisted. The flowers are borne on long, slender stems and most artistic.

MRS. J. W. WILKINSON—Deep pink, with very long petals. 50c each.

GEN. BULLER—Rich, velvety crimson-maroon, tipped white. 25c each.

W. B. CHILDS—A beautiful, dark purple-maroon. 35c each.

RENE CAYEUX—Clear, glowing crimson. Early and profuse bloomer. 35c each.

Dahlia, Frank A. Walker. One half actual size

Decorative Dahlias

This type produces large, somewhat flat but most beautiful flowers, double and full to the center; petals irregularly situated, long, broad and nearly straight. A beautiful and most popular type.

COUNTESS OF LONSDALE—Salmon-pink, a good variety. 50c each.

ELIZABETH SLOCOMBE—Rich, deep garnet; fine, large flowers; extra good stems and a strong, vigorous grower. 50c each.

EASTON—Brilliant Turkish red, good form and remarkably free flowering. 35c each.

J. M. GOODRICH—New decorative. Color is entirely new and wins instant favor. A beautiful salmon-pink, each petal effectively tipped primrose-yellow. 50c each.

JACK ROSE—The identical shade of the rose with the same name. 25c each.

MINOS—Intense, velvety maroon, almost black. Ideal cut flower variety. 25c each.

FRANK A. WALKER—A charming shade of deep lavender-pink. For garden decoration or for cut flowers has no superior. Flowers are produced in abundance on long stems. 25c each.

GLORIANA—Beautiful pure gold color, slightly reddish towards center. 75c each.

Peony Flowered Dahlias

Gorgeous new type, semi-double, loosely arranged petals, two, three or more rows in the flower, surrounding a large golden-yellow center, petals pointed, sometimes twisted, and sometimes the inner ones curl over the center, like a Peony. The artistic flowers are very large, flower freely and are borne on long, strong stems, making them excellent for cutting as well as garden decoration.

CALIFORNIA—In color it is a beautiful clear, rich, deep yellow. The blossoms are large and produced upon good, long, stiff stems. 50c each.

HORTULANUS BUDDE—A bright scarlet of splendid habit. 25c each.

ROCHESTER—Color a gorgeous crimson-maroon, effectively striped and splashed pure white. Every petal twisted, making a gay contrast with the yellow center. Excellent stems for cutting. 50c each.

29

Hardy Hybrid Perpetual Roses

This class is noted for its extreme hardiness. Especially adapted to northern climates. Known as the old-fashioned "June Rose." Large flowers. Deliciously fragrant.

*Frau Karl Druschki

The best hardy, snow-white rose now known. Tremendously strong grower. Hardy anywhere; immense, glorious flower, snow white in color.

*GLOIRE LYONNAISE—Flowers large and full; color white, base of petals canary. Tea scent.

*HUGE DICKSON—Flowers large, of fine form, opening well. Color brilliant crimson-shaded scarlet. Sweetly scented.

*PRINCE CAMILLE DE RO-HAN—Deep velvety crimson-maroon, full and of good form and the best of all hardy dark Roses of this class.

*HIS MAJESTY — Color deep, dark crimson, shaded deep vermilion-crimson towards the edges A most remarkable Rose.

*GENERAL JACQUEMINOT —Known everywhere as the famous "Jack" rose; crimson scarlet, very fragrant, large, full.

*ULRICH BRUNNER— Cherry red Immense in size, beautifully formed

*CAPTAIN CHRISTY—Delicate peach-blown pink. Deeper in center. Large, full.

* Green Rose—A Curiosity

A most interesting member of the rose family, grown for its oddity. Flowers are small, pointed, double, and of the same color as the foliage—dark pea green.

* Sir Thomas Lipton Rugosa Rose

A handsome double Rugosa Rose, with the peculiar leathery foliage of the family and beautiful snow-white, exceedingly fragrant flowers borne on long stems. Hardy as an oak.

Great White American Beauty—Frau Karl Druschki

Henri Martin Hardy Moss Rose

Deep rosy-carmine shaded to bright crimson. A most charming large rose with exquisitely mossed buds.

Price of all roses on this page: Strong, first size pot-plants, 30c each, any 4 for $1.00, postpaid; extra heavy two-year-old plants, soil on roots, 85c each, $9.00 per dozen assorted, by express; prepaid by parcel post, 95c each. varieties marked * can be furnished in star size or specimen plants at $1.00 each, by express; prepaid by parcel post, $1.15 each.

Practical Garden Books

COMMERCIAL ROSE CULTURE (by Eber Holmes)—A fine work. **$2.50 postpaid.**

GARDEN GUIDE—How to plant and maintain the home grounds. Vegetables and flowers, 336 pages, profusely illustrated. Postpaid, paper cover, **$1.00.**

GARDENING FOR PLEASURE—Especially written for amateurs, 404 pages, illustrated. Price, **$2.25, postpaid.**

PRACTICAL LANDSCAPE GARDENING— The result of twenty years of practical experience. Containing sketches, plans, etc. Postpaid, cloth cover, **$2.65.**

MILADY'S HOUSE PLANTS—With the aid of this book anyone can have a fine collection of blooming plants to add cheer and beauty to the home during the fall and winter months. Postpaid cloth cover. **$1.10.**

Better Plants and Gardens

INSECTICIDES AND FERTILIZERS

VIGORO A specially prepared plant food for gardens, lawns, flowers, shrubbery. The proper feeding of the plant is very important, and its growth, vigor and beauty are governed largely by the kind of plant food furnished. It is without unpleasant odor and is agreeable to apply. Shipped by express. Price, 25 lbs., $2.50; 50 lbs., $4.00; 100 lbs., $7.00.

FAMOUS HORTOGEN PRODUCTS

Fertilize Through the Foliage

FUNGTROGEN

A highly concentrated fungicide that conquers Mildew and controls Black Spot on roses, Phlox and other plants, and is an effective plant stimulant, as well. ½ pint, 85c, postpaid.

INSECTROGEN

For leaf-chewing insects—caterpillars, slug worms, Japanese beetles, etc., and blights. A powerful fertilizer. Used alternately with Fungtrogen. Both carry their own spreader. ½ pt., $1.10, postpaid.

APHISTROGEN

Destroys the destructive aphis in two or three applications. For all plants subject to aphis or plant lice. All these sprays carry the noted Rosenbluth leaf fertilizer — Hortogen. Complete with spreader ready for use. Simply mix with water. 4 oz., 85c, postpaid.

FEROGEN

Spring-Summer Ground Dressing and Ground Stablizer. A valuable plant food. Reinforces manure fertilizer. Supplies essential chemical elements to the soil. 1 lb. tins, 90c; 2 lb. tins, $1.50, postpaid.

TEROGEN

Autumn-Winter Ground Dressing. Destroys the spores of fungi of most diseases. Kills the larvae of insects, such as rosepith, borer, rose bugs, Japanese beetle, aphids and ants. A valuable fertilizer. 1 lb. tins 90c, postpaid.

HUDSON HAND SPRAYER

The Perfect Vaporizer

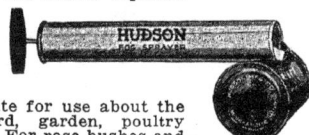

A favorite for use about the home, yard, garden, poultry house, etc. For rose bushes and flowering shrubs. Made of heavy tin, capacity ¾ pint. **Price. 90c, postpaid.**

TYRIAN PLANT SPRINKLER

is essential to success with plants. With it you can quickly sprinkle them. It will keep the foliage fresh and healthy. Throws a spray "just like rain." Postpaid, 90c each.

SULPHO-TOBACCO SOAP

For sure, easy and immediate extermination of all insect life on plants, trees and animals, Sulpho-Tobacco Soap is a matchless preparation. Will not injure the most tender plant. It dissolves readily in water, and may be applied with a Tyrian Sprinkler. Price, 3 oz. cake, 15c; 8 oz. cake, 30c, postpaid.

SPECIAL OFFER—The "Tyrian" Sprinkler and a 3 oz. package of Sulpho-Tobacco Soap for $1.00, postpaid.

STIM-U-PLANT TABLETS

An excellent, odorless, highly concentrated plant food, tablet form, for all kinds of pot plants during the winter. Will increase growth and heighten color. These can be used in tablet form or dissolved in water. Complete directions with every package. Price, small size, 25c; 100 tablets for 75c; 1000 for $3.50, postpaid.

WALKER'S EXCELSIOR PLANT FOOD

comes as a boon. It is so simple, the good results so positive that there is no reason why any flower lover should be without a box of this, the essence of plant life. It is an odorless preparation, combining every element required in plants to produce vigorous, healthy growth and profusion of flowers.

2½ oz., making 3 gals., postpaid, $0.25
5 oz., making 6 gals., postpaid, .45
12½ oz., making 15 gals., postpaid, .70

Charming Gladioli

The gladiolus is growing more popular each year, both blooming in the garden and for use as a cut flower. Our list is not large, but comprises the very best varieties, all guaranteed to bloom this year. Our bulbs are not the usual one-year size too often sent out at low prices, but large, healthy, sure-to-bloom, two and three year old bulbs, full of vitality, ready to start growing when planted. All gladioli are sent by mail, postpaid, at the prices mentioned. Selected from hundreds of the best varieties. In size of flowers, blooming quality and diversity of color none will compare with these.

ANNIE LAURIE—Lavender pink, petals beautifully ruffled.

E. J. SHAYLOR—Tall; beautiful, pure deep rose-pink.

EVELYN KIRTLAND—Rosy-pink, brilliant blotches on lower petals; tall spike.

HERADA—Pure mauve. Very beautiful.

JEWEL—Light salmon, yellow blotch.

CRIMSON GLOW—A perfect, very large, deep scarlet-crimson.

MAIDENSBLUSH—Very early, light pink. A great favorite.

LE MARECHAL FOCH—Rose-pink. An improved America. Large flowers and very early.

LOUISE—Beautiful deep lavender.

PRINCE OF WALES—Flowers are large and color is most charming coral pink.

SCHWABEN—Clear canary-yellow shading to soft sulphur. Large flower stalk and wonderful blooms.

MRS. FRANCES KING—Brilliant vermilion scarlet.

Price of named varieties of Gladioli, 15c each; $1.50 per dozen, postpaid.

SPECIAL OFFER—One each of the entire set of the 12 splendid gladioli, in strong, sure to bloom bulbs, $1.50 postpaid.

SUPERFINE MIXTURE

All colors gladioli, large bulbs, sure to bloom, 50c per dozen, $3.50 per 100, postpaid.

Fine Tuberoses

DWARF EXCELSIOR PEARL— Flowers pure white, very double, of immense size and sweetly scented. 5c each; 50c per dozen, postpaid.

ORANGE-FLOWERED—Bears snow white flowers. 7c each, 75c per dozen, postpaid.

NEW VARIEGATED-LEAVED — The leaves are bordered with white; large, white flowers. 7c each, 75c per dozen.

SPECIAL OFFER—We send postpaid, six Excelsior Pearl Tuberoses, three Orangeflower-er and three New Variegated-leaved—twelve in all for 50c.

Charming New Castle Gladioli

Handsome Large Flowering Carnations

There is no plant that grows in the garden that is more attractive or handsome than the carnation; our extra strong, stocky plants will bloom all summer and produce in wonderful abundance their large, superb flowers which have exquisite clove fragrance. Bring indoors in early fall. Grown in pots the plants will bloom continuously during the winter.

New Castle Carnations

Best Carnations

Price, strong pot plants 15c each, any 6 for 75c; $1.50 per dozen, postpaid.

AVIATOR—The best standard crimson on the market.

MRS. C. W. WARD—Fine, deep pink, very fragrant.

ROSE-PINK ENCHANTRESS—Large, deep pink.

MATCHLESS—Clear, brilliant white, fine form and very large. Highly scented. A very delightful variety.

RADIUM—New, handsome red. Fine, large bloom.

Decorative Ferns

There is a charm about the fern for home ornament hard to equal with any other plant, with its long sprays of fresh, lively, green, handsome foliage. Even the smallest plants will in a short time grow into magnificent specimens. They are of the easiest culture, requiring little or no care, and will last indefinitely. They like partial shade.

WHITMANII—This is a condensed form of the "Ostrich Plume Fern," with valuable characteristics added which are not evident in the parent. Very graceful.

BOSTON FERN—Long, broad fronds, drooping gracefully; forms an immense plant.

TEDDY, JR.—New dwarf fern. Fronds are broad and beautifully tapered from the base to the top, drooping just enough to make a graceful plant.

ROOSEVELT—New and grandest of all, with fronds beautifully frilled and waved. Compact, vigorous grower.

SCOTTI—Dwarf growing, compact and a great favorite. Broad petals, strong, upright plant.

EXALTATA—Strong, upright grower; deep green fronds of heavy texture.

Price of all ferns: Strong, shapely plants 20c each; any 6 for $1.00, postpaid; larger size, 4 and 5 in. pot-plant, 85c each by mail, postpaid.

ASPARAGUS SPRENGERI—For pots, vases or hanging baskets. The long, slender branches droop most gracefully, clothed with feathery, emerald green fronds. **Price, 20c each; 3 for 50c, ppd.**

ASPARAGUS PLUMOSUS—Foliage resembles the finest lace. Elegant for cutting. **Price, 20c each; 3 for 50c, postpaid.**

Fern Whitmanii

33

Charming Baby Rambler Roses

Dainty, dwarf-growing Polyantha Roses, excellent for bedding clumps single specimens or for pot culture. Hardy, healthy and always blooming. Immense clusters. Exquisitely beautiful.

* Geo. Elger

This superb Polyantha Rose produces great quantities of lovely little buds of golden yellow, opening into miniature symmetrical Roses. Each bush is so loaded with blooms that they resemble a huge bouquet. Grand grower, blooming all summer. Very hardy.

WHITE BABY RAMBLER (Catherine Zeimet)—Pure white flowers borne in immense clusters. Most delicious fragrance—that of cherry blossoms. Exquisite.

*CRIMSON BABY RAMBLER—Color clear, brilliant ruby red; foliage dark and glossy; blooms every day in the year, but grows only twenty inches high. Better than an Azalea; it is superb for single specimens, dwarf hedges and bedding.

*THE LOVELY ANNY MULLER—Much the same as the Crimson Baby Rambler except in the color of the flowers, which are a shiny and brilliant pink, produced in the greatest profusion in large clusters.

*MLLE. CECILE BRUNER—Rosy-pink on rich creamy white ground; a great bloomer.

*MARIE PAVIE—Medium size, very full and double; borne in large clusters; white flushed with carmine.

*MISS EDITH CAVELL—Recommended as the best, bright crimson with white eye; enormous clusters; strong growing; very dwarf in growth; extraordinarily beautiful.

*IDEAL—The darkest of all the Baby Ramblers, an intense lustrous garnet. Flowers are not large but are produced in very large trusses and are very effective. Compact habit of growth. Blooms abundantly all season.

Beautiful **Crimson Baby, Edith Cavell**

Price of all Roses on this page: First size plants, 25c each; any 5 for $1.00; two-year-old plants 80c each; $8.50 per dozen assorted; prepaid by parcel post, 90c each. Varieties marked * furnished in still larger plants, star size $1.00 each, by express, charges collect; prepaid by parcel post, $1.15 each.

Gives an idea of mass effect of White Baby Rambler

Hardy Shrubs for Permanent Planting

They are absolutely hardy, and, once planted, last indefinitely, increasing in size and beauty year after year. For cold climate where hardy plants are needed, they stand out without an equal. Planted in clumps, masses or used for hedges, screens, or for filling unsightly corners, they make a glorious show. They supply that certain something which is lacking in every yard where hardy shrubbery is not planted. We recommend a liberal planting of this class of plants. They last a lifetime and are sure to give splendid satisfaction.

Some varieties, such as Hydrangea, Snowball, Weigelas, Deutzias, require pruning in early spring before new growth starts. Here with us it is done in late February or early March each season.

New Everblooming Hydrangea

Hydrangea Paniculata Grandiflora

They are extensively used for yard, lawn and hedge planting and for screens. Attains a height of 5 to 7 feet; hardy in all localities; blooms the first and every season in July and August, and continues in bloom for two or three months; the flowers are massive, cone-shaped, often measuring 10 inches in length, and have a pleasing variation of color, changing from original pure white to pink, and finally to beautiful, rich, coppery-red. Well rooted, field-grown plants.

Price, Hydrangea Paniculata Grandiflora and New Everblooming: Strong, well rooted first size field grown plants, 50c each; 6 for $2.50 postpaid. Larger field grown two and three year old, $1.00 each, $10.00 per doz. by express; $1.15 each, $11.00 per doz. by parcel post prepaid.

New Everblooming Hydrangea

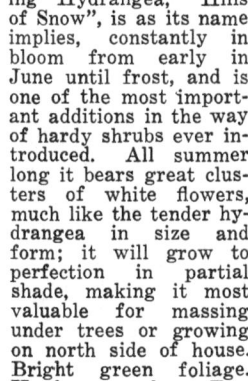

This New Everblooming Hydrangea, "Hills of Snow", is as its name implies, constantly in bloom from early in June until frost, and is one of the most important additions in the way of hardy shrubs ever introduced. All summer long it bears great clusters of white flowers, much like the tender hydrangea in size and form; it will grow to perfection in partial shade, making it most valuable for massing under trees or growing on north side of house. Bright green foliage. Hardy everywhere. Tremendously popular. (*See color illustration page 44*).

Hydrangea Paniculata Grandiflora

Geraniums

These old favorites continue to be the most popular of flowering plants. Scarcely a home anywhere is without Geraniums. Easy to grow, lasting indefinitely, always blooming, both indoors and in the open ground there is nothing to take the place of Geraniums. Our list includes the finest varieties in cultivation. We offer large, well-developed plants for immediate blooming.

A. BROWN—Magnificent rosy crimson; beautiful.

FRAU PERKINS—Beautiful cerise pink, white center.

MAD. BARNEY—Famous double pink, of a lively shade; exquisite.

LA FAVORITE—Double, pure white. The leader.

ALPHONSE RICARD—Double, bright vermilion.

JEAN VIAUD—Double, bright, clear shade of mauve-rose, shading to a clear white throat.

S. A. NUTT—Double, dark red. Free bloomer. None better.

SCARLET BEDDER—Scarlet.

IMPROVED POITEVINE—Salmon pink. Very free flowering.

RED BARNEY—Red; strong grower.

Geranium, S. A. Nutt

SPECIAL OFFER
One each of the 10 flowering geraniums above, in extra large, thrifty plants, $1.60, postpaid.

Price all Geraniums, large, thrifty plants for immediate effect. 20c each; 6 for $1.00, $2.00 per dozen, in one or assorted varieties, postpaid.

Giant Persian Cyclamen

Giant Persian Cyclamen

The most beautiful and decorative of all pot plants. The foliage is dark olive-green, beautifully variegated with silver and rose. The fairy-like flowers are carried on long stems, produced for several successive months. The flowers, which are of odd form, embrace every delightful shade of color and are a distinctive feature of this handsome house plant. We offer splendid strong plants ready to bloom, assorted colors, our selection, at 50c each; 3 for $1.25, postpaid.

The plants I ordered this spring from you are thriving very well.—Thomas J. Shortall., St. Johns, Newfoundland.

36

Gorgeous American Beauty Peony

Heller's Magnificent Peonies

Of all the flowers in the hardy garden, the Peony is easily recognized as the queen—in fact, it vies with the rose for that title in many ways, for while in bloom it is without question the most glorious object in the garden. Once Peonies are planted they last for a lifetime. They stand the severest winters without the slightest protection. After blooming their charm lies in the beauty of their foliage, for even when not in bloom the Peony plant is decorative in the extreme and well worthy of a prominent place in the garden.

New and Rare Peonies

LIVINGSTON—Rose type, late very full, compact pale lilac rose with silvery tips, center flecked carmine. **$2.00 each, postpaid.**

GROVER CLEVELAND—Very large, compact, rose type. Dark crimson. Strong grower, late. **$2.00 each, postpaid.**

KARL ROSENFIELD—Semi-rose type. Midseason. Very tall and compact grower of stately habit. Fine bloomer. Brilliant dark crimson. **$3.00 each, postpaid.**

SUZETTE — Semi-rose type. Midseason. Handsome flowers of elegant shape and superb coloring. Bengal rose shaded carmine purple with silvery reflex. **$2.00 each, ppd.**

DR. H. BARNSBY—Large, full, globular blooms. Soft solferino red shaded crimson with pronounced bluish reflex; late **$3.50 ea.**

MIXED PEONIES—60c each; **$7.00 doz. ppd.**

Select List of Peonies

EDULIS SUPERBA—Red, very large, double.

FESTIVA MAXIMA—White center, flaked red, double, early.

AMERICAN BEAUTY—Immense, brilliant crimson. Nothing to equal it.

DUCHESS D'ORLEANS—Dark carmine.

QUEEN VICTORIA—Best white.

CANDIDISSIMA—Double. Creamy white.

CHARLEMAGNE—Lilac; white, slight blush center. Double.

MODESTE GUERIN—Deep rose. Double.

FRANCOIS ORTEGAT—Deep crimson.

CANARY—Double. White primrose center.

Price all Peonies, except where noted, in large two and three eye roots, 85c each, $9.50 per dozen postpaid, assorted as desired.

HARDY SHRUBS (Continued)

Deutzias

Valuable self-sustaining shrubs which vary considerably in height and habit, but bloom alike in dainty bell or tassel-shaped flowers, borne thickly in wreaths along their branches, in June. The taller sorts are useful for specimens, groups, and the background of shrubberies; the dwarfer, for borders or for planting near the house.

CRENATA—4 to 6 feet; double white, tinted rose.

PRIDE OF ROCHESTER—4 to 6 feet. Pure white, with a faint blush.

Weigelas

Beautiful shrubs that bloom in May, June and July. The flowers are produced in so great profusion as almost entirely to hide the foliage.

CANDIDA—Snow-white flowers. late June.

LAVELLEI—Deep red flowers; beautiful.

ROSEA—Flowers are large and of a deep rosy color. One of the best.

Spireas, Meadow Sweet

All the spireas bloom with a riotous extravagance which makes them quite striking. Their individual style, color and habits of growth differ so markedly that a collection of varieties will insure bloom the entire season.

PRUNIFOLIA (Bridal Wreath)—Double white flowers.

VAN HOUTTEI—The bushes form compact clumps. Pure white flowers, borne in great masses.

ANTHONY WATERER—Perpetual blooming crimson spirea. Makes a low, compact bush, 15 to 18 inches high. Large heads, deep crimson flowers.

Prices of all Deutzias, Weigelas, Spireas: first size plants, field grown, 35c each; 3 for $1.00, postpaid. Two-year-old field-grown plants, 75c each; $8.50 per dozen by Express; 85c each; $9.50 per dozen, postpaid.

California Privet

The One Best Hedge Plant Combining Beauty Hardiness and Efficiency

For many years we have made a specialty of growing California privet for hedges, and our stock cannot be surpassed anywhere. It is strong, thrifty and in the best shape for transplanting. Each one a specimen plant. We have it in all sizes, from one-year-old plants to large, vigorous bushes, which can be used with telling effect in the formation of an immediate hedge. These large plants are the most economical to buy, for with them the tedious years of waiting for the hedge to grow will be avoided.

PRICES CALIFORNIA PRIVET

First size, 12 to 14 inches, 6 for 50c, postpaid; $6.00 per 100 by express. Second size, 2 to 3 feet, 3 for 50c, postpaid; $10.00 per 100, by express or freight at purchaser's expense. (Orders for 50 filled at 100 rates.)

Berberis Thunbergi (Barberry)

Grows 3 to 4 feet high; small, perfectly shaped, rich green leaves, turning in autumn to bright scarlet. Flowers a delicate shade of coppery yellow, followed by beautiful, brilliant red berries, clinging all winter. Strong thrifty grower, soon making a luxuriant effect.

Price Berberis Thunbergi, first size plants, 20c each; 6 for $1.00, postpaid; $12.00 per 100 by express; larger plants, 50c each, $5.50 per dozen, by Express; $35.00 per 100, express or freight. (50 at 100 rates.)

Spirea Van Houttei

38

HARDY SHRUBS—Continued

Meehan's Marvel Mallow

Philadelphus Grandiflora
MOCK ORANGE
A very desirable free-blooming shrub. Sweet scented, pure white flowers with yellow stamens. Blooms first year.

Double Japan Snowball
VIBURNUM PLICATUM
Blooms in early June, when the whole bush is loaded down with great, compact balls of pure white, double flowers. They are borne in such profusion that the entire plant appears one dense mass of bloom; the tree grows erect and bushy, 6 to 8 feet high, with deep green leaves peculiarly crimped and crinkled. Wondrously beautiful.

Price of all shrubs offered on this page: First size, field-grown plants, 40c each, prepaid. Two year old sizes, 75c each; $8.50 per dozen by express; 85c each, $9.50 per dozen, prepaid, by parcel post.

Buddleia
BUTTERFLY BUSH
This is perhaps one of the most popular of our Hardy Shrubs. The long flower spikes are made up of numerous small florets somewhat on the order of a Lilac. The color is a beautiful shade of lilac shading to lavender, and the plant is a mass of bloom from June until frost. It is perfectly hardy and increases in size and vigor each season.

Althea
ROSE OF SHARON
Purple. The flowers are brilliant and striking. B.ooms during August and September at a season when there are few other blooming shrubs. Height 9 to 12 feet when matured.

Forsythia
GOLDEN BELL
Bright yellow bell-shaped flowers. The first spring flowering shrub. A spreading bush with dark shining foliage. Blooms before the foliage appears and is covered by its wealth of bloom.

Hibiscus
MEEHAN'S MARVEL MALLOW
Large flowering plants which make a bush-like growth from 4 to 5 feet high and 2 to 3 feet across. The flowers are enormous in size, frequently 8-10 inches in diameter. Mixed colors—pink, red or white.

Double Japan Snowball in full bloom

Nº1

Nº2

Nº3

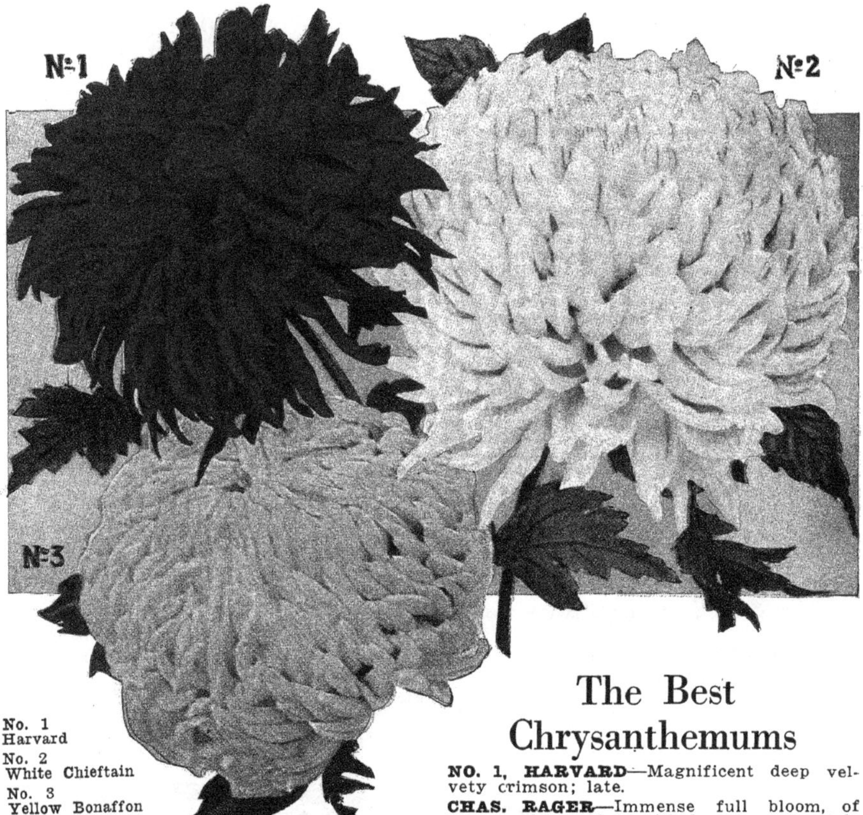

No. 1
Harvard

No. 2
White Chieftain

No. 3
Yellow Bonaffon

Hardy Chrysanthemums

After roses, Chrysanthemums are our leading specialty. There is nothing so easily grown. They make a magnificent show blooming in early September and continuing until severe cold weather in December; they produce their gorgeous flowers in lavish abundance and grow to perfection in ordinary soil with a fair amount of sunshine. If large specimen blooms are wanted pinch off the buds, except the ones you want to develop. Hardy with protection except in extreme cold climates.

Pompon Chrysanthemums

These are entirely hardy and produce hundreds of medium size, perfectly double flowers, making an excellent show. Last until late in the autumn.

KLONDIKE—Gorgeous yellow; free bloomer.

MRS. BUCKINGHAM—Single, rosy pink.

DIANA—The best pure white; late.

GOLDEN FEATHER—Grand, new, yellow.

LILLIAN DOTY—Beautiful shell pink.

The Best Chrysanthemums

NO. 1, HARVARD—Magnificent deep velvety crimson; late.

CHAS. RAGER—Immense full bloom, of purest white color, with large waxy petals well incurved..

UNAKE—Grand incurved, beautiful lavender pink of good shape and fine size.

BETSY ROSS—Mid-season to late, incurved white.

WHITE FROST—Beautiful white, perfect ball shaped. One of the choicest.

YELLOW FROST—Light yellow, straight petals.

NO. 3, YELLOW BONAFFON—Beautiful in form; bright yellow, standard of its color.

NO. 2, WHITE CHIEFTAIN—Pure white, beautiful ball-shaped flowers; good in every way, lasting well when cut.

PACIFIC SUPREME—Extremely large, rich pink.

GOLDEN GLORY—Bright golden yellow, immense, perfect flowers, early. Superb.

ROMAN GOLD—Superb, early, yellow, perfect.

Price of all chrysanthemums on this page: Strong plants, 15c each, any 4 for 50c; $.150 per dozen assorted, postpaid.

40

Wonderful Canna Lilies

We offer these popular flowering foliage plants in started pot-plants only. No one need go outside of this list to procure the last word in Canna Lilies. Wherever a gorgeous effect is wanted there is nothing to equal the Cannas; with their magnificent banana-like foliage they impart a tropical aspect to the lawn or garden and there is no plant to compete with them wherever luxuriant, gorgeous effects are wanted. The foliage of itself is majestic, while the flowers come in immense heads and throughout the entire summer they are a blaze of glory. Dig and store away during winter in a fairly dry, moderately cool, frost-proof cellar.

Price on all Cannas, except where noted, strong thrifty pot-plants, 25c each; 6 for $1.25; $2.50 per dozen, postpaid.

PRESIDENT—Considered by al to be the best red variety yet introduced! Produces immense heads of glowing crimson flowers, 7 inches across the open bloom on strong, erect stalks well above the foliage; 4 feet.

PANAMA—The unusual color marking of this new canna is its attractive feature. The orange-red petals are bordered with a broad edge of golden-yellow. Flowers large and overlapping. Free bloomer.

KING HUMBERT—A glorious canna. The finest we have ever seen. Grows to a height of about 5 feet. Immense dark bronze foliage; great heads of orange-scarlet flowers, striped crimson.

YELLOW KING HUMBERT — Green foliage, large blooms yellow, dotted red, five feet in height.

WINTZER'S COLOSSAL—4 feet. The immense gorgeous, vivid scarlet blooms produced all summer long. Blooms reta n their color during the hottest weather.

MRS. ALFRED F. CONRAD—4 feet. One of the largest introductions. Color a beautiful shade of salmon-pink. Flowers of immense size. Producing blooms so freely as to make a continuous show for several months.

AMERICAN BEAUTY — Height 5 ft. Said to be the richest colored Canna known, a velvety carmine cerise. With its large flower heads is unusually attractive. Every stalk produces two heads of bloom well above the soft green foliage.

CHARLES HENDERSON—Brilliant crimson, 5 feet.

GIGANTEA—Tall growing, 7 feet, bronze foliage, medium crimson flowers. $12.00 per 100 by express.

NEW YORK—Giant scarlet, foliage plum color, 5 feet.

WYOMING—Orange, immense, seven feet.

ALPHONSE BOUVIER—Beautiful wine red, distinct, five feet.

Canna Bed No. 26
FOR CIRCULAR BED 4 FEET ACROSS
1 Red for center.

CANADA. The ten plants ordered from you arrived, very nicely packed and in good order.—Frances Kearns, Outremont, Que., Canada.

Old Fashioned Flowers—Perennials

There is a constantly increasing demand for the old favorites in the gardens of long ago, and more and more the flower-lovers are filling their gardens with hardy perennials—the kind that live from year to year, inncreasing in size and beauty until they fairly run riot with their wealth of bloom and glory of form and color. Hardy.

VIOLETS—For richness and modesty the violet is supreme. Before the last snows are gone this modest flower shyly appears out of its icy bed, telling of the coming of spring.

California—The largest violet in cultivation. Rich violet-blue.

Lady Hume Campbell—Double, blue.

Swanley White—Pure white, perfectly double.

ACHILLEA (The Pearl)—Double white flowers produced in large sprays all summer. Fine for cutting.

HOLLYHOCKS—Double, mixed colors.

COREOPSIS—A gem among hardy plants. It begins to flower in June and continues in bloom more or less throughout the season. Flowers are of a golden yellow, of graceful form and invaluable for cutting. Succeeds in any position.

GAILLARDIA (Blanket Flower) — Among the most attractive and effective of our hardy perennial plants. Will thrive in almost any position or any soil. One mass of bloom from June till autumn. The gorgeous flowers, 2 or 3 inches in diameter, dark red, brown in center with bands of crimson-orange and vermilion, are borne on stems 18 to 24 inches long.

LUPINS—Produce beautiful long spikes of pea-shaped flowers a foot long on stems three feet high.

Hollyhocks   Coreopsis   Gaillaridia

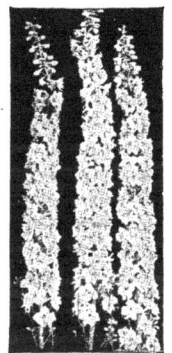

Delphiniums

DELPHINIUMS (Hardy Larkspur)—One of the most popular perennials, excellent for cutting. Fine, large flowers. Mixed colors.

CAMPANULA (Canterberry Bell) — Choice mixed. Large clusters of bell-shaped flowers.

PYRETHRUM (Painted Daisy)—Pyrethrums are of low, compact growth with lace-cut foliage of beautiful green and are excellent for edging, or for general planting and in solid beds. The flowers resemble that of a Daisy in shape, are of large size, and the color ranges from pure white and the various shades of pink and red to deep purple.

IRIS—Offered elsewhere. See page 44.

STATICE—Produces immense panicles of delicate blue flowers. One of the best perennials for cut flowers, either fresh or dried for winter bouquets.

AQUILEGIA (Columbine) — As a cut flower the Long-Spurred Columbines are the daintiest of all outdoor grown flowers. They are a most important part of every hardy garden. Mixed colors.

ORIENTAL POPPY—Brilliant crimson-scarlet with black blotches at base of petals. Beautiful and showy.

PHLOX—See page 48 for list of varieties and prices.

DAY LILY (Hemerocallis)—

Gold Dust—Large, clear yellow flowers, rich.

Thunbergi—Sweet scented, clear, full, rich yellow flowers in July.

DIGITALIS (Foxglove) — Gorgeous spikes of tubular flowers. Grows four to five feet tall in majestic effect.

SWEET WILLIAM—For many years the Sweet William (Dianthus Barbatus) has been considered one of our finest hardy garden plants, being of easy culture, thriving in any good garden soil and lasting for years.

Fox Glove

SHASTA DAISIES—These are universally popular for outdoor planting and considering their many good qualities there is no cause for surprise to see them planted so extensively. The flowers are of the purest, glistening white, of enormous size and produced on long stiff wiry stems, which make them excellent for cutting purposes.

DIANTHUS (Pinks)—All colors. Their fragrance, perfect form and rich coloring make them great favorites for edgings, walks and drives.

Price of all hardy perennials on this and opposite page, strong, well-rooted plants; 25c each; 5 for $1.00; $2.25 per dozen, postpaid.

These perennials will live and flower for many years, and require very little attention after planting.

Oriental Poppy

Phlox

Aquilegia

43

German Iris

The memory of the "Blue Flag" of the old-time gardens is one ever sweet to those whose lives were lived in such surroundings, while the "modern" Irises, if we may use the term, will remind one of the old days; they, too, like everything else these days, have yielded to the influence of improvement. Hardy everywhere and permanent, growing larger year after year.

CAPRICE—Cerise, deeper falls, early.

CATERINA—Standards light blue, falls lilac; very large; very tall.

CRIMSON KING—Rich claret purple.

DR. BERNICE—Standards coppery bronze falls rich velvety crimson. Extra.

HONORABILIS—Golden yellow and crimson brown.

MADAME CHEREAU—White frilled edges beautifully penciled violet-blue.

QUEEN OF MAY—Lilac pink, large; midseason. Beautiful tall growing variety.

SPECIOSA—Lavender purple and reddish purple.

SHERWIN WRIGHT—Fine bright yellow

WALHALLA—Standards light violet, falls deep purple.

Price of all Iris: Strong plants, 20c each; 3 for 50c; set of 10 varieties above, $1.50 postpaid.

Iris, Caprice and Honorabilis

New Everblooming Hydrangea

The New Everblooming Hydrangea "Hills of Snow" is, as its name implies, constantly in bloom from early in June until frost, and is one of the most important additions in the way of hardy shrubs ever introduced. All summer long it bears great clusters of white flowers, much like the tender hydrangea in size and form.

Price, strong, 1st size plants, 50c each; 6 for

New Everblooming Hydrangea

Hardy Phlox

We have no more satisfactory flowering plants than hardy perennial Phlox. Once planted they are permanent. Hardy as oaks. Require no protection, no petting, no coaxing. Free from disease and insects. Have immense heads of blooms of the most brilliant and delicate colors, which are produced in continuous profusion until cut down by severe freezes. Ordinary garden soil is all that is necessary. They are indeed the glory of the summer garden. We offer strong hardy plants for immediate blooming. Our list is the best now known.

ATHIS—Clear salmon pink.

EUROPEA — White with red eye. Flowers and trusses large.

INDEPENDENCE—Pure white.

LA VOGUE—Silvery Rose.

PANTHEON—Fine bright pink.

PROF. VIRCHOU—Carmine.

RHEINLANDER—Salmon pink.

R. P. STRUTHERS—Carmine.

THOR—Ruddy salmon pink.

VON HOCHBURG—Blood red.

Prices Hardy Phlox: Strong, vigorous field-grown plants, the only reliable kind for immediate effect, 30c each, 4 for $1.00; $2.90 per dozen, postpaid. One each, 10 Phlox above, $2.35, postpaid.

Phlox Rheinlander

Hardy Climbing Vines

ENGLISH IVY—A splendid evergreen climber, with dark, glossy green leaves; clings firmly to stone, brick or wood walls without trellis or support. 25c each; 5 for $1.00, postpaid.

AMPELOPSIS VEITCHII (Boston or Japanese Ivy)—It covers buildings and walls with a perfect mat of dark green, leathery foliage, which changes to brilliant crimson as fall approaches. Clings to either tree or wood without support. Fine plants, 25c each; 5 for $1.00; three-year-old plants, 75c each, postpaid.

CLEMATIS PANICULATA—The flowers are pure white and are borne in great panicles or clusters of bloom, fairly covering the plant, so that it is a mass or sheet of fleecy white with an exquisite fragrance. It begins to bloom late in August the first year. Hardy in all seations of the country. Strong pot plants, 25c each. Strong two-year-old, field grown plants, 50c each, postpaid.

WISTARIA ALBA—Flowers pure white in pendulous clusters. 25c each; 5 for $1.00, postpaid.

WISTARIA MAGNIFICA — The finest wistaria of its color now known. Extremely vigorous, growing 30 to 40 feet in one season when well established. The flowers are pale lilac, and the immense clusters of drooping racemes, which measure 12 to 18 inches in length, are deliciously fragrant. 25c each, 5 for $1.00 postpaid.

45

ILLINOIS. Roses purchased from you last spring have all grown wonderfully and have far surpassed our expectations for beautiful bloom and foliage. Out of all our roses we lost only one.—Mrs. Herbert Burtar, River Forest, Illinois.

Important—How To Order

Terms Cash With Order. Personal check, Post Office Money Order, Bank Draft, Express Money Order, Registered Letter, all may be sent at our risk. Stamps accepted in small amounts only.

Please Use Order Blank and write name and address plainly. Write letters only when necessary and then on a separate sheet.

Parcel Post and Express Shipments. All goods priced post paid are usually sent by parcel post, prepaid. All goods sent by express are shipped at purchaser's expense. Shipments by parcel post may be insured against damage and loss for eight cents extra, to be remitted with order. This will insure up to $25.00 in value.

All Orders Shipped Immediately upon receipt, unless directed to the contrary. Ordering early is a great help, and we gladly reserve stock for future delivery when desired, if you will give shipping date.

Foreign Orders. Twenty-five per cent extra should be added to orders going outside the United States proper, to pay extra cost of packing and postage. To countries with which we have a parcel post, goods can be sent by mail.

Canadian Customers. Canadian laws permit sending all plants into Canada at any time, but a permit must be secured from the Secretary of the Destructive Insect and pest Advisory Board, Department of Agriculture, Ottawa. Owing to the rate of postage on Canadian orders we must request an additional 25 per cent to cover postage.

We reserve the right to substitute another variety of equal value for any variety the stock of which may be exhausted, unless we are instructed to the contrary.

Heller Bros. Co. is a trade name. The sole owner of this business is P. J. Lynch.

Our Guarantee. All shipments in the U. S. A. Proper (does not include Canada

and U. S. Colonial possessions) must satisfactory when received or order w be duplicated or money refunded, whic ever you prefer, but you must advise of your wishes within ten days after t receipt of the shipment. After delivery good condition our responsibility ceas If complaints are not made in ten da we can not entertain them. We give guarantee, expressed or implied, as quality or productiveness of any plan or bulbs we send out; and while we stri to have our plants true to name, we not guarantee it. Soil and climatic con tions work changes in colors of many ros which no one can explain. Frau Ka Druschki, purest white rose, will som times come light pink. Jeannette Hell will appear almost pure yellow, then aga almost white, again deep pink; flowe will be lacking in petalage. Soil con tions, wet or dry growing seasons, la frosts, improper care, lack of water, t much water, an unfavorable location— dozen causes may be responsible for fa ures that do occur over which we ha no control, hence we desire to make pla our responsibility and terms under whi our goods are sold.

Different Sizes in Roses

As to which size rose plant is most desirable depends largely upon how much money you wish to spend. All sizes are good and produce splendid results. All are pot-grown.

First Size Rose Plants will produ wonderful results, both in growth a profusion of flowers, even the first ye of planting. We have sold millions of the and their popularity is increasing becau they give wonderful satisfaction.

Two-Year-Old Rose Plants are mu larger in size, and as we grow them her in blooming capacity and quality, are t best and cheapest rose plants in Americ Pot-grown, always on own-roots and full foliage when sent out.

Star Size Rose Plants are larger in si than the average two-year-old. Th character of plants originated with u They are the last word in size and bloo ing capacity.

To Whom It May Concern:—"Mr. P. J Lynch, owner of Heller Bros. Company, stands high in the buisness community and does an extensive nation-wide business. We recommend him as an honorable, upright business man, whose guarantee may be relied upon at all times."

Citizens State Bank, New Castle, Ind.

Our roses being pot-grown may be planted a time during the growing season, no matter money you live. There is no "closed planting season with our pot-grown rose plants. They are rea for shipment whenever you are ready to pla them.

HOW TO USE

STIM--PLANT

PLANT STIMULANT TABLET

Odorless—Clean—Convenient
Acts Immediately—No Waste

Simply insert tablets in the soil. Or, if a solution is desired, dissolve four tablets in a gallon of water. Apply directly to the soil—not on leaves or stems.

A tablet every two weeks—until three or four have been used—will make cucumbers, squashes, and melons, fairly jump.

In hills, for other plants than vines, use one tablet to each hill.

In flower-beds and borders, place tablets one foot apart.

On bush fruits and shrubbery, use two to four tablets, placed in the soil about each plant.

Good also for coldframes, hotbeds, greenhouse benches, and pot plants.

Dahlias and Gladiolis will be greatly benefited by inserting two or three tablets in the ground in a radius of about 4 inches from stem.

Lawns—one tablet to gallon of water.

For all potted plants, insert half a tablet in soil approximately every ten days.

For roses, place two or three tablets in soil every ten days or two weeks during period you wish to stimulate them.. The effect will be magical.

Every plant, flower, bush, tree, vine, or vegetable growing anywhere will be wonderfully benefited by Stim-U-planT.

BUY IT OF

HELLER BROS. COMPANY

Growers of the

"Famous Roses of New Castle"

NEW CASTLE, INDIANA

INDEX

page we give a complete alphabetical list of all the Roses offered in this book, showing
which they belong, and the page on which they are described. Abbreviations used:
ooming Teas; H. T., Hybrid Teas; H. P. Hardy Perpetuals; C. T., Climbing Teas;
dy Climbing; M., Moss; Pern., Pernetiana; P., Polyantha; Rug., Rugosa C. H. T.,
ybrid Teas.

General Index of Plants, Bulbs and Garden Supplies

cial Bargains in Roses, Chrysanthemums and Plants see insert
between pages twenty-four and five.

CPSIA information can be obtained
at www.ICGtesting.com
Printed in the USA
BVHW050036061118
532207BV00022B/2670/P

9 780656 604432